SERMONS ON THE BEATITUDES

SERMONS ON THE BEATITUDES

John Calvin

Five Sermons from the *Gospel Harmony*,
Delivered in Geneva in 1560

Translated into English by
ROBERT WHITE

THE BANNER OF TRUTH TRUST

THE BANNER OF TRUTH TRUST
3 Murrayfield Road, Edinburgh EH12 6EL, UK
P.O. Box 621, Carlisle, PA 17013, USA

*

First published in French as part of the *Soixante cinq
sermons sur l'Harmonie ou Concordance des trois
Evangelistes,* Geneva, 1562

First Banner of Truth edition, 2006

© Robert White 2006

ISBN-10: 0 85151 934 2
ISBN-13: 978 0 85151 934 0

*

Typeset in 11 /15 pt Adobe Caslon at
the Banner of Truth Trust, Edinburgh
Printed in the U.S.A. by
Versa Press, Inc.,
Peoria, IL

CONTENTS

INTRODUCTION

*A*mong the many activities which claimed Calvin's attention during his long ministry in Geneva (1536–38; 1541–64), preaching was the most public and perhaps the most influential. Public because, for many years, twice on Sundays and daily in alternate weeks, the Reformer stood before a congregation of townsfolk, refugees and visitors to teach, warn, appeal, counsel, admonish, and encourage. Influential because, vital as the *Institutes,* commentaries and treatises were to the defence and propagation of Christian doctrine, it was the Word preached and applied from the pulpit which above all fashioned Geneva's evangelical culture and made it the nerve-centre of Reformed Protestantism.

The sermon is, in itself, an unrepeatable event, localized in time and space. It must be recorded, transcribed, preserved and transmitted if it is to have any impact beyond the limits of the assembly to which it is addressed. A large number of Calvin's sermons were in fact recorded and preserved in manuscript form and subsequently turned into print. This is not the place to repeat what has been written by others regarding the history of Calvin's sermons.[1] It is enough to note that, whatever the preacher's reluctance to allow unedited sermon collections to be published and sold, the competence of his stenographer and copyists, the clamour of his printers and the enthusiasm of his reading public were such that, happily for us, he relented. Almost 1600 sermons, on both Old and New Testament books, exist in the original French, and over one hundred more have survived in Latin translation. Almost half of

---

[1] The best discussion in English is that of T. H. L. Parker, *Calvin's Preaching* (Edinburgh: T. & T. Clark, 1992), pp. 65–71.

the extant sermons were published in Calvin's lifetime, and over the last forty years a major publishing initiative by the World Presbyterian Alliance has made available hundreds more which have long lain unread in various European libraries.[2] English-speakers have been fortunate in having had, since Calvin's time, access to a large portion of the Reformer's homiletic works in translation. A calculation of the number of sixteenth-century works in translation reveals that it was the English and Scots who constituted Calvin's most avid foreign readership.[3]

The present volume seeks to present readers with a short series of sermons on the Beatitudes, translated for the first time into English, and comprising Calvin's exposition of Matthew 5:1–12, Mark 3:13–19 and Luke 6:12–26. Five sermons were preached on the Beatitudes in the course of an extended treatment of the Synoptic Gospels. Begun in July 1559, the series on the Synoptics had still not been completed by February 1564, when ill-health forced the Reformer's retirement from the pulpit. His absence was to be permanent: he died three months later, in May 1564.

The groundwork for a systematic study of the first three Evangelists had been laid in 1555, when Calvin produced a commentary, in both Latin and French, on *A Harmony of the Gospels*. The idea of grouping parallel Gospel passages so as to form a harmony or concordant narrative was not new, since Bucer, the Strasbourg Reformer, had earlier adopted the device in his commentary on the Synoptics (1527). Calvin was happy to acknowledge his debt to Bucer in the preface to his own commentary.[4] Exegetically, the

---

[2] Eight volumes have appeared to date in the *Supplementa calviniana* series, Neukirchen-Vluyn: Neukirchener Verlag , 1936/1961–2000.

[3] T. H. L. Parker, *Calvin's Preaching*, pp. 71–73; Francis Higman, 'Calvin's Works in Translation', in Andrew Pettegree, et al. (eds.), *Calvinism in Europe, 1540–1620* (Cambridge: Cambridge University Press, 1994), pp. 82–99.

[4] *A Harmony of the Gospels: Calvin's New Testament Commentaries*, ed. D. W. and T. F. Torrance (Edinburgh: St. Andrew Press, 1972) I, p. xiv.

sermons follow much the same lines of interpretation as are found in the commentary. They differ from the commentary, however, in their more elaborate and nuanced exposition of the biblical text, and in their insistent application of its message to a Christian audience, which, while of its own time, is also of ours. Their late date marks them out as a definitive example of the Reformer's mature pulpit style. They represent his very last effort to elucidate a New Testament text in the context of regular public worship.

By a poignant coincidence, the sermons on the Beatitudes were also the last to be recorded by Denis Raguenier, Calvin's remarkable stenographer. With Matthew 5:12, Raguenier laid aside his pen and prepared himself for death, which came to him in the winter of 1560-61. While the preacher continued to work his way through the Synoptics, no further record now exists – if one ever did – of his subsequent exposition.

The Beatitude, as a literary genre, belongs to both the wisdom and the apocalyptic traditions. It may therefore be used as a vehicle of ethical instruction, inculcating certain norms of behaviour, or as a vehicle conveying to the distressed hope and assurance that God will intervene to right all wrongs. In his sermons Calvin gives great weight to the ethical demands implicit in the Beatitudes of Matthew 5:1-12 and Luke 6:20-23. Expressions of obligation ('we should', 'one must', 'it is necessary to') and of moral exhortation ('let us') abound. He does not, however, treat the Beatitudes as entrance requirements to the kingdom announced by Jesus, but rather as marks whereby those who are already in the kingdom may be discerned, and God's grace to them made visible in a fallen world. In actual fact the Beatitudes contain only one explicit command, which speaks not of moral effort but of inner, mental disposition: 'Rejoice and be glad' (*Matt.* 5:12), 'Rejoice and leap for joy' (*Luke* 6:23). Eschatological hope lies at the core of Jesus' teaching here: the grieving *will* be comforted, the hungry *will* be satisfied, the pure *will* see God. As preacher, Calvin is fully alert to the tension which exists between the *now* and the *not yet*, between believers' present experience of suffering and their future exaltation in heaven. As Jacques Dupont has remarked, 'The Beatitudes are simply another way of saying that "the kingdom of God is here", that God's promises are on the point of being fulfilled, that the appointed beneficiaries of the messianic blessing at the end of time may now rejoice, for the time is accomplished.'[5] Jesus is both the herald and the agent of the messianic blessing. All the Beatitudes are summed up in him. Meek, pure in heart, merciful, peaceable, persecuted without cause, he enacts his own message and thus becomes the very embodiment of all righteousness. His vindication will be the vindication of all who believe in him. The Beatitudes thus send us back, not to an abstract list of moral perfections, but to the person of Jesus Christ, to whose image Christians are even now being conformed by his indwelling Spirit. Calvin's sermons on the Beatitudes are an appeal and an encouragement to Jesus' followers to be what they are already reckoned to be in him.

The sermons translated here formed part of the collection *Soixante cinq sermons sur l'Harmonie ou Concordance des trois Evangelistes*, published in 1562 by the Genevan printer Conrad Badius – a thick octavo volume of some 1200 pages. Amongst other things it incorporated the preface which Calvin had written for his commentary of 1555. The *Soixante cinq sermons* appeared later that year in a separate edition by Lyons printer Symphorien Barbier, who no doubt wished to capitalize on Calvin's popularity in his native France.[6] Apart from a reissue in 1590 of the Badius edition, under

---

[5] J. Dupont, *Les Béatitudes* (Paris: J. Gabalda, 1958–73) I, p. 221.

[6] A full description of the 1562 Geneva and Lyons editions is given by Rodolphe Peter and Jean-François Gilmont, *Bibliotheca calviniana* (Geneva: Droz, 1991–2000) II, pp. 953–60.

a false title page, no further publication followed until the late nineteenth century, when the Strasbourg scholars Baum, Cunitz and Reuss included the *Soixante cinq sermons* in their monumental edition of Calvin's collected works (*CO*).[7]

The Reformer preached on the Synoptics in the course of the Sunday services held in the main church of Geneva, St Peter's. The Ecclesiastical Ordinances which governed the city's church life provided for two Sunday services, morning and afternoon. In the Genevan liturgy the sermon, preceded by a call to worship, a general confession, sung metrical Psalm, and prayer for illumination, was followed by an extended intercessory prayer and the benediction. Few of Calvin's sermons are less than an hour in length, and some are longer. Yet although the sixteenth-century churchgoer might speak of attending the sermon rather than divine service,[8] the fact remains that the exposition of Scripture was a liturgical act, an act of worship, designed not only to instruct the mind and to nourish godliness but to warm the heart and to lift it in gratitude to Father, Son and Holy Spirit.[9]

The sermons on the Beatitudes are numbered 61 to 65 in the original edition. They are closely printed, without paragraph divisions. At the head of each sermon is the preacher's text (cited according to the 1562 edition of the Geneva Bible). Marginal notes identify the Scripture references which Calvin uses by way of illustration but for which he does not often give chapter and verse. The text of the improvised prayer with which the sermon concludes is

---

[7] W. Baum, E. Cunitz and E. Reuss (eds.), *Calvini opera quae supersunt omnia*, (Brunswick/Berlin, 1863–1900) 46.1–826.

[8] Cf. Francis Higman, 'La Fortune de la *Forme des prières* en Grande-Bretagne jusqu'au milieu du XVIIe siècle', in Maria-Cristina Pitassi (ed.), *Edifier ou instruire: les avatars de la liturgie réformée du XVIe au XVIIIe siècle* (Paris: Honoré Champion, 2000), p. 78.

[9] See, on the general question of church and worship, Richard Stauffer, *Interprètes de la Bible* (Paris: Beauchesne, 1980), pp. 157–64.

also given. None of the *Soixante cinq sermons* is dated. Internal evidence, however, suggests that they were delivered in the space of a month in the autumn of 1560. By a happy chance the preacher identifies two Psalms sung (according to a prescribed order) in the course of the services, allowing a precise calculation to be made of the interval between his first and last sermon. If Rodolphe Peter is right in dating the last sermon (Sermon 65), 17 November 1560, the first sermon (Sermon 61) – an afternoon sermon, as we will see – may reasonably be dated 20 October.[10] Such a chronology accords well with what we know of the Reformer's circumstances in his last years. His preferred pattern of two Sunday sermons on consecutive texts could not always be maintained in the face of heavy outside commitments, and of the recurring bouts of ill health which had affected him since 1558.

The *Calvini opera* of Baum, Cunitz and Reuss still provides, despite its limitations, the best and most convenient access to Calvin's writings.[11] I have based my translation on the text of the *Soixante cinq sermons* printed in *CO* 46, but have cross-checked with the text of the Badius edition of 1562 whenever a reading appeared faulty or problematic. I have endeavoured to render Calvin's thought faithfully, but without always reproducing those elements of his spoken style which are merely repetitive or, as is often the case, redundant.[12] The syntax of the sermon text is occasionally defective, and from time to time some reordering of the sequence of clauses has been necessary in the interests of coherence. Some over-long periods have been shortened, paragraphs (absent in the Badius edition) have been introduced, and punct-

[10] R. Peter and J.-F. Gilmont, *Bibliotheca calviniana* II, p. 954. On the significance of the sung Psalms, see endnotes to Sermons 1 and 5.

[11] Cf. F. L. Battles, 'The Future of Calviniana', in Peter De Klerk (ed.), *Renaissance, Reformation, Resurgence* (Grand Rapids: Calvin Theological Seminary, 1976), pp. 139–40.

[12] On Calvin's spoken style, see T. H. L. Parker, *Calvin's Preaching*, pp. 139–49.

uation modernized. The term 'papist', unpleasant to the modern ear, has been retained. Calvin uses it to designate not so much the totality of Roman Catholic believers as the Roman controversialists with whom he constantly crossed swords, and the hierarchy who, intermittently since 1545, at the Council of Trent, had been occupied defining doctrine and anathematizing Protestant dissent. On both sides of the confessional divide, polemic was conducted along the severest of lines.

Overall, my objective has been to allow readers to *hear* the Reformer speaking on issues of perennial Christian concern in a modern idiom. Calvin does not, of course, preach in a vacuum. His mind ranges widely over Old and New Testament Scriptures. It is Psalms in the Old and Romans and John's Gospel in the New which he most frequently invokes, but often in the vaguest of terms: 'as we read in the Psalms', 'as St Paul declares'. The device of endnotes (signalled in the text by numbers) has been used to identify Bible references, some of which appear as marginal notes in the Badius edition but which are missing in *CO*. Endnotes have also been used when the sermon text calls for a brief historical or theological comment. At the head of each series of endnotes I have inserted a short analysis of the sermon's main features.

The sermons on the Beatitudes have been renumbered 1 to 5, and have been provided with titles descriptive of their content. The Scripture texts on which each sermon is based (almost certainly supplied by Raguenier or his copyist) are translated direct from the French, as are those cited by Calvin in the course of his sermon. It will be seen that, frequently, the preacher quotes from memory or else paraphrases, so that no two citations of the same text are necessarily identical.[13]

[13] Cf. Max Engammare, 'Calvin connaissait-il la Bible? Les citations de l'Ecriture dans ses sermons sur la Genèse', *Bulletin de la Société de l'Histoire du Protestantisme Français* 141 (1995), pp. 163–84.

A translation is not, in itself, a critical edition. No attempt has been made to identify the expositor's sources, either ancient or modern, or to examine his use of exegetical tradition. In the endnotes I have been concerned to point to parallels, or to suggest contrasts, with other commentators only in a few cases. Doubtless Calvin's sources are the same as those used for his commentary of 1555: principally Augustine, Chrysostom, and Jerome among the ancients, Erasmus, Melanchthon, Bucer, and Bullinger among the moderns. Given the liturgical context in which the Sunday sermon was placed, I have included at the end of each sermon the improvised prayer which Calvin's nineteenth-century editors chose to omit. It restates, often with wonderful conciseness, the sermon's leading themes. The prayer for illumination which Calvin pronounced immediately before the Sunday sermon, and which was patterned on his practice in the Strasbourg church, prefaces the sermons printed here. The long, set prayer of intercession which followed the sermon, appears after Sermon 5.[14]

I am grateful to Jean-François Gilmont for advice regarding the dating of Calvin's sermons, and to the staff of the Bibliothèque Nationale de France and of the Bibliothèque de l'Histoire du Protestantisme Français (Paris), for access to their rich sixteenth-century collections. The Badius edition of the *Soixante cinq sermons,* which I consulted for purposes of comparison, is one of three copies held by the latter library (Rés. 8^0 5752). I express my sincere thanks to the Banner of Truth Trust and to the editorial staff for their warm welcome and encouragement.

ROBERT WHITE

April 2006

[14] Details of the Genevan liturgy and its Strasbourg antecedents may be found in R. Peter's introduction to Calvin, *Sermons sur les livres de Jérémie et des Lamentations, SC* 6, pp. xxv-xxxix. A useful older study is that of William D. Maxwell, *The Liturgical Portions of the Genevan Service Book* (London & Edinburgh: Oliver & Boyd, 1931), pp. 17–47.

PRAYER BEFORE THE SERMON[1]

*L*et us call upon our good God and Father, beseeching him, since all fullness of wisdom and light is found in him, mercifully to enlighten us by his Holy Spirit in the true understanding of his Word, and to give us grace to receive it in true fear and humility. May we be taught by his Word to place our trust only in him and to serve and honour him as we ought, so that we may glorify his holy name in all our living and edify our neighbour by our good example, rendering to God the love and the obedience which faithful servants owe their masters, and children their parents, since it has pleased him graciously to receive us among the number of his servants and children.

[1] The Genevan liturgy of 1542 allowed, in the Sunday services, for a prayer of illumination to be said by the minister immediately before the sermon, but prescribed no set form of words. Calvin's practice was to use a prayer which he had already employed in the French church of Strasbourg, and which was modelled on Bucer's German liturgy. Text in *CO* 23. 741-2; cf. *OS* 2. 19-20 (see p. 87 for these and other abbreviations used in the notes).

I

CALLED AND CHOSEN

Then he went up on to a mountain, and called whom he wished to him, and they came to him. ^{14} And he set aside twelve to be with him, and to send them out to preach, ^{15} and to have power to cure sicknesses and to cast out devils. ^{16} The first was Simon (to whom he gave the name Peter). ^{17} Then there were James, the son of Zebedee, and John the brother of James (whom he called Boanerges, which means 'sons of thunder'), ^{18} and Andrew, and Philip and Bartholomew, and Matthew and Thomas and James the son of Alphaeus, and Thaddaeus and Simon the Canaanite, ^{19} and Judas Iscariot, who also betrayed him (Mark 3:13–19).

It happened in those days that he went away into a mountain in order to pray, and he spent the whole night in prayer to God. ^{13} And when it was day, he called his disciples, and he chose twelve whom he also named apostles. ^{14} These were Simon, whom he called Peter, and Andrew his brother, James and John, Philip and Bartholomew, ^{15} Matthew and Thomas, James the son of Alphaeus, and Simon surnamed the Zealot, ^{16} and Judas the brother of James, and Judas Iscariot, who also turned traitor. ^{17} Then, coming down with them, he stopped on a plain with the whole company of his disciples and with a great crowd of people from all of Judaea and Jerusalem, and from the coastal area of Tyre and Sidon. These had come to hear him and to be cured of their

3

*sickneses. [18] And those who were tormented by unclean spirits
were cured. [19] And the whole crowd sought to touch him, for power
was coming forth from him, and he was curing all of them*
(Luke 6:12–19).

O ur Lord Jesus Christ in the fifteenth chapter of St John,[1]
desiring to instil in his disciples an attitude of humility and
fear, and to give them no opportunity for pride, tells them that it
is he who has chosen them, not they who have chosen him. In
effect he says that his grace has gone before them, and that they
have not attained this honour through their own efforts. This is
what St Mark alludes to when he declares that Christ chose *whom
he wished.* It is therefore not for us to inquire why the twelve who
are mentioned here were favoured above all others in the group.
Our Lord already had many disciples who freely followed his
teaching, yet they are left to one side as private individuals while he
takes only the twelve. It is pointless to ask whether Peter was more
powerful than another, or James more eminent, or John more
worthy: that would get us nowhere. In fact such speculation is
given short shrift when Mark tells us that Jesus Christ chose those
whom he willed, thus demonstrating that we have no right to
insist he tell us what prompted him to act this way. We must
instead rest content with the choice he made, even if we cannot
understand the reason behind it.

How, indeed, can we explain our soul's salvation except in terms
of God's good pleasure and his free gift of mercy? For if we think
that we are better than others whom he has passed over or abandoned, we simply demean God's unconditional kindness through
which we obtain salvation. And this we do every time we seek to
gain a measure of importance or esteem in men's eyes. Every
mouth must of necessity be shut. We must learn that God has
chosen us, not because he saw something good in us, or found us

more amenable than those whom he rejects, but simply that he might reveal the full splendour of his generosity.

That, then, is how the apostles' ministry came about. It is quite clear that, had our Lord Jesus Christ wished to choose people suitably gifted for such a task, none would have been found. The very angels in paradise would not have sufficed. How could poor, perishable creatures like us bring anything to such a work? That is why the Lord Jesus had here to exercise his Father's prerogative of mercy, of which he was the agent. And that will be much plainer to us when we see that he chose poor fishermen, ignorant men who had never set foot inside a school and who could not, as the saying goes, tell A from B.

When afterwards he called others, he chose them not from the city of Jerusalem or from the esteemed ranks of the priestly caste; he chose men who were unknown, men who up until then had counted for nothing. We will later see how St Matthew was called – busy at his money-desk, a tax collector loathed by everyone. If we sought to discover why Christ preferred to have him as an apostle rather than men of higher rank, that, as I said before, would get us nowhere. So pay careful attention to St Mark's statement, that the Lord *took those he wanted*. This, I say again, should curb every sort of conjecture and speculation; we should not aspire to know more than is proper about God's works, nor intrude further than we should into his counsels.[2] Let us simply accept that what he does accords perfectly with the standard of equity, wisdom, and righteousness, even though such things are beyond our knowledge.

So much for the first point. There is a second point to note. Human beings are nothing; they can give nothing to God which makes him accountable to them. As Scripture says, 'Who first gave him a gift, that he should return the favour?'[3] For if we want God to esteem us, we must have something which is ours to offer. But if he has no particular duty or obligation toward us, what charge could we possibly bring against him? The simple fact is that every-thing we have is ours only because he gave it to us. So we, our persons and everything he has put within us belong to him; we are accountable to him for them. What is more, he needs nothing from us, and none of our works can reach to where he is, as Psalm 16 says.[4]

We conclude then that when God calls us to positions of promi-nence or responsibility, he does so of his own good pleasure, and not, as we imagine, because he considers us more capable than others. His aim is to humble us, by showing that everything depends on his grace and not on human merit. Now if that is true of temporal preferments, how much more does the principle apply to our eternal salvation! When God adopts us as his children in order to make us members of our Lord Jesus Christ and sharers in his heavenly glory, what credit can men possibly claim for them-selves? And if they do make such a claim, do they not deserve to lose everything because of their ingratitude? That, then, is another point worth noting.

In these verses both St Mark and St Luke allude to events which concern the later history of the twelve. At any rate they do not imply that Christ had already ordained them apostles. (That we shall see in due course.) It is, however, with the expectation of apostleship that they have been set aside. Here, then, is a select group of twelve men from among the disciples who, when the time was ripe, would be usefully employed. But to begin with they were not commissioned as apostles, nor was the task of gospel preach-ing immediately assigned to them. Nevertheless our Lord accepted them as his servants. Thus they came, yielding him such obedience as would prepare the way for the later apostolic order. In naming them apostles, he had regard to their future commission, not to their present calling. In short, we observe that Christ set the twelve apart so as to train and, as it were, polish them. We plainly see that they were rough men, for although they received instruction before ever they opened their mouths, they were so ignorant and obtuse that we blush to see how little they learned from the Son of God, who is the source of all wisdom, the light of the world. What if he had straight away sent them out? How could they have proclaimed the message which was later entrusted to them – the message of salvation? They could not have rightly uttered a single word!

So now we understand our Lord's intention: to prepare the chosen twelve to be apostles, in advance of the commission he was to give them, and about which more will be said. Yet even then he will tell them that, as apostles, his aim is not to make them consummate teachers, but rather trumpets signalling the arrival of the one who is to speak. The apostles served therefore as heralds, bidding men listen to Jesus Christ, accept his teaching and prepare the way, which, as we saw, John the Baptist had already done. However, the apostles' commission was not at first so broad as John the Baptist's; it only became so after the resurrection. But that must be left for another time.

We see then that, as I was saying this morning,[5] our Lord Jesus Christ did not fulfil the office of master, prophet, and teacher merely while he walked on earth; he would do the same work in future times, making provision for his church lest it lose the doctrine of salvation. This shows us how greatly he cares for the salvation of all who belong to him. For the twelve were chosen, not simply for the sake of those who were alive then, but for our sake too, so that we today might still enjoy the benefit of their teaching. Today, then, Peter's example of steadfast zeal shows us the way of salvation; today, too, the voice of John, called the 'voice of thunder', rings out on every hand. Both should touch us to the quick.

Understand, therefore, that Christ had in view the onward movement of the gospel, intending not only that we should hear it from his own lips, but that there should be others to preach reconciliation with God his Father after his death and resurrection. This was his purpose in choosing the men named here.

Our text goes on to say that *he withdrew to a mountain to pray, and remained in prayer all night long*. Here we will only touch on the matter of prayer, leaving a more thorough treatment to a more appropriate time.[6] It is true that our Lord did not need to pray on his own account. Since, however, he was head of the church, and since he was subject to all our infirmities except sin (being without blemish), and since he took our nature and was truly joined to us, it was necessary for him, being our brother, to pray. Indeed, he set us an example in prayer. It would be quite wrong to think that prayer for him was a mere pretence, and that he simply showed us what to do without being touched by any sense of need. We will see in due course how determined he was in the matter of prayer. Do we display such intensity and fervour that when we call upon God we sweat blood and water? That is what will later be said of him. If we weep when we petition God in prayer, do we not show that we are truly stirred, and that this is no sham, but that necessity compels us? We read in the eleventh chapter of St John that Jesus shed tears when he brought Lazarus back to life.[7]

In short, whenever Scripture says that Jesus Christ prayed, we must conclude that he not only humbled himself but became, for our salvation, as nothing. As nothing – that is the term which St Paul uses to describe him.[8] Now if our Lord had resigned himself to a position of middling rank, that in itself would have been something to wonder at. But in choosing to be subject to all our infirmities, in taking them upon himself except, as I have said, for our evil desires (for nothing in him was contrary to God's righteous law: he was free from sin and the very appearance of sin) – what a token of love was this, love without limit! We see, then, in all this, how necessary prayer was for him. So when he comes to choose his disciples he asks God his Father to direct him and to guide his choice. For here he is acting in his capacity as man; as God, such a thing could never be. But as our head he is so much one with us that what is ours becomes by transfer his; always and everywhere he is our model.

It was necessary, then, that God should direct the choice he was to make. That is why he prayed so earnestly. Not as we are accustomed to pray, carelessly and as a mere formality: he spent the whole night in prayer. Notice how this rebukes our own lazy and cold practice of prayer. We imagine that we are doing wonders when we pray morning and night; we feel we are being suitably spiritual despite the many distractions which get in our way. But it is a very different pattern which our Lord sets for us here. He keeps watch until daybreak, concerned and in distress of soul until he finds rest in God, laying before him his many cares for the church.

If we chose to argue that what Jesus did was unique to him, we have only to see what David says about himself, or how St Paul – speaking not in order to boast, but to instruct believers everywhere – spent night and day upon his knees before God.[9] Let us therefore learn to discipline ourselves when we feel lethargic and have only half a heart for prayer – or worse, when the will to pray is but one-tenth or one-hundredth of what it should be. Let Christ's example be a spur inciting us to amend our leisurely approach to prayer. At the very least let us groan before God, asking him to forgive our faults; for these might shut the door to him, deny us access, and prevent our prayers being answered.

This is what we should say: 'Lord, I am a poor, wretched creature, and am unworthy to look up and to seek anything from you. Nevertheless you continually take me by the hand. Your reach is wide. Although I am far from you, do not withhold your grace from me. Despite all I have done, extend your boundless power even to me, and hear my request.' That, then, is another truth to be gleaned from this passage.

Scripture goes on to say that *he called to him Simon Peter and the children of Zebedee*. It is true the text has 'Boanerges', but we should read 'Benai reges', that is, 'sons of thunder'. Such changes are not uncommon. For when a proper name in our language is translated into another, it is often not exactly rendered, as in Peter's case, when he is called Cephas. That is not what Christ originally called him, for what resemblance is there between the names Cephas and Peter? Taking the Greek and Latin word, there is a great difference between 'Peter' and 'Petré', as he would have been called.[10] So we should not be overly surprised if a syllable or two has changed. The Gospel writer specifically explains the nickname given to John and his brother James.

Now it is true that all the apostles might properly be termed 'sons of thunder'. As the prophet Haggai says, at the preaching of the gospel heaven and earth are shaken and the whole world trembles.[11] Peter was an ambassador of the gospel no less than James and John, yet he was not called by that name. Nevertheless the Lord Jesus Christ means particularly to show here how he will work in James and his brother John. By the same token the term 'Peter' may be applied to all believers, as the apostle himself says when he urges us to be built as living stones into God's church, each stone resting on the foundation already laid, which is Jesus Christ. St Peter clearly shows what he and all God's children have in common: as living stones they serve to build the spiritual body which is the church. However, he rightly bears the name, as one chosen to display such constancy and courage that we might draw strength from his example.

Observe that our Lord has no intention here of praising the apostles for qualities which might be thought of as their own. How could James and John have impressed anyone by their thunder? They were always on the water, addressing their remarks to mute sea-creatures, to fish, no less! In themselves they possessed none of the qualities attributed to them here. The same is true of Peter. We know how grievously he later fell, and he would have stumbled many times more had not the Holy Spirit from on high sustained him by his power. In Peter there was nothing but infirmity; he was weak as water, and would have fainted in an instant. The title which our Lord assigns to him simply anticipates the power he was to give him. The same may be inferred of Zebedee's children. They were called 'sons of thunder', not because they spoke with the same powerful effect as thunder – as we heard a moment ago in the Psalm, where God so thunders as to cause the deer of the forest to miscarry, the trees to topple, and the mountains to shake.[12] No, John and James were very ordinary men, poor ignorant souls who would have blushed to appear in polite society; by no stretch of the imagination could they be termed 'sons of thunder'. But when he called them by that name, Christ at the same time endowed them with that gift. In brief, we see that he had no desire to make idols of these three disciples, or to suggest that what was attributed to them came from within themselves. He meant us instead to see his goodness at work in them, so that we might more readily exalt the riches of grace bestowed on him by the Father. As well, it is clear that, in seeking to make use of Peter, Jesus gave him an honourable title in order to enhance his disciple's authority. The same is true of James and John.

Today, therefore, when we read what Peter has left us by way of teaching, we can be sure that we will be firmly grounded in God's truth and will never be moved; our faith, though tried, will remain unshaken. And however constantly the devil may assault us, we must nevertheless hold to God's unchanging truth, since Peter, minister of God's truth, bears the name which bids us never waver. When also we read John's Gospel or Epistles, we should be stirred up to receive what they contain in fear and reverence. There, to be sure, we discern John's thunder. No man alive could possibly rival him in the excellence of his teaching. And if we were not so dull-witted, we would certainly be enchanted by every word he writes. This, then, is the real significance of the apostles' titles. They have important lessons for us, because they are meant to authenticate for us the teaching laid down by Peter, James, and John.

At this point, the question might be asked: How did the Lord Jesus Christ come to choose Judas Iscariot? If we reply that he did not know the kind of man he was, Jesus could be said to have prayed in vain, his prayer to the Father being unanswered. That is patently absurd! As we will see later, he knew how faithless men could be. It was not then error or negligence which made the Lord choose him. Why, then, did he place him among the sacred band of apostles whom, he asserts, he has chosen to be judges and leaders of Israel – twelve heads, as it were, over the twelve tribes? How strange of him to appoint Judas, a thief and traitor, the mirror image of wickedness, to such a position!

Observe first that it was important for us to be armed and equipped against the scandals which meet us every day. We tend to be shocked when we see God allowing wicked men to rise to prominence in his church, and to pose as pillars of the Christian faith, until, that is, their godlessness is revealed. When God is said not only to allow such things but actually to bring them to pass, we might well object (supposing we had the right to do so): 'What? The church is called God's temple: nothing unclean must enter it, it must be without spot or blemish. How can God allow things to be so tainted and defiled when only angelic purity and perfection will do?' That is the kind of judgment we make when we rely on our own understanding. God, however, schools us by other means. The church – such is his will, as we will later see – is like a net which gathers fish both good and bad, or like a threshing-floor where straw is mixed with good grain.[13] In essence, that is why these things exist. But what if we can see no reason for them? We

should nevertheless submit to God's ordinance: to look for expla-
nations is a waste of time. The fact is, as St Paul says concerning
heresies, these things must be, so that those who are truly approved
by God may be plainly revealed.[14] Why, you ask? When everything
is properly run, and when both great and small are united in serving God, what impostors there are will be shamed into acting
properly. They may even claim – as we will later see – to be among
the most spiritually advanced. But when troubles and hindrances
occur, those with no vital root of faith or robust fear of God within
them will seize their chance to create the utmost mischief.[15] If a
false doctrine is preached, some who before professed to be agreed
on every issue will lend a sympathetic ear to heretics. Or if an evil-
doer seeks to disturb the peace and good government of the
church, there are those who will throw all caution aside and shout
their support for him. That, then, is why God wills that his church
should be mixed, and that the wicked, scoffers, worldly and immoral should be mingled with the honest and believing.

Such things are not confined only to the common people; they
happen too among the leaders, among men of prominence: they
are meant to serve as salutary lessons. It is written of the Antichrist
that he will sit in God's sanctuary.[16] In the same way St Paul says
that among the pastors and those called to this office, there will be
many greedy wolves ready to devour the flock. Even when addressing those whom he himself has called and chosen, he declares:
'From among you and your company, such men will come.'[17] That,
then, is how God seeks to test our steadfastness and the integrity
of our faith. He gives Satan free rein to sow confusion in his
church. At the same time his aim is to keep us humble, and to
prompt us to pray for deliverance from all that would cause us to
stumble or would lead the world to ruin. We would soon drift into
indifference if we thought the world was getting better and better:
we would cease to value prayer or to look to God for aid. When,

however, forced to mix with evil-doers and scoffers who cause such offence among us, we realize the misery of our condition, we cannot help but sigh and pray for an end to confusion, for God to exercise control, to prosper the work already begun, to ratify and continually confirm it.

This is what we have to remember here. Judas was chosen as one of the apostles so that, if anyone among today's leaders should stumble, we might nevertheless continue steadfast and obedient to God. It would be a mistake to rely on men, and to say: 'Just imagine! A man we all thought of as a pillar of the faith has betrayed us! He has thrown over the doctrine which for years he professed and become an apostate! What can we cling to now, and where should we turn for assurance?'

It is to prevent this kind of distress that Judas is placed here before us. He was chosen to be an apostle, yet he stumbled and was lost. For all that, the church remained firm, protected by the power of God's Spirit. So then, when we see some fall who were once reputed to be little angels, understand that God will have mercy on his people, and that what St Paul says in the second chapter of 2 Timothy is true.[18] If we call upon God's name and are separate from sin, this is his stamp of approval: our Lord Jesus Christ knows those who are his. He keeps them with his seal upon them, to show that they are in safe hands. We should remember, too, what Jesus promises in the tenth chapter of St John – that of all that he has received from the Father, nothing will perish. He will take good care of them all, until the last day.[19]

I come to my next point. When we see men fall like this, we should be warned to look carefully to ourselves. For St Paul, in a passage where he is speaking about the Jews, says that all who stand should beware lest they fall.[20] We are therefore warned to remain modest and humble when we see people who were much further on than we are, cut off from the church. Our attitude should be: 'Alas! The same could have happened to us, except that God wonderfully preserved us by his grace!' Note that point.

Note also that those who attain a place of honour should put all pride aside. Let them remember that any fall would prove far more fatal than if they had chosen obscurity. For, as is often said, when a man falls from his natural height, he can get back on his feet; but if he falls from a roof or a high window, he is past all help.[21] If God in his mercy were to draw us to his side and to set us apart from the crowd, we would be like men on a stage, visible to everyone. If we were to fall from there, it would be much worse than if we were mere nobodies. That too is a thought worth pondering. For when we read that Judas not only kept Christ company but was himself an apostle – a much more important role – and that nevertheless he was called a devil,[22] what can we say?

At the very least we should learn not to blame God for the sins of men. If we had nothing more than Judas' example to go on, the office of apostle would today be an object of mockery. Worse, we would feel disgust when told that someone no better than a devil was in fact an apostle. But where would that get us? We are all too ready to grumble at what Scripture is saying here. Be sure of this, that the very worst of human guilt can never affect God's settled purpose. What exactly do I mean? Supposing magistrates and judicial officers are corrupt and evil, bent on perverting the social order, twisted and vile, dissolute in the way they live. When we see such men, tyrants who rob and swallow up the weak, must we conclude that the office they hold is impaired, and that the honour and prestige which God has attached to it are flawed? Not at all! However much men defile themselves with evil, they cannot touch the things which are of God. These remain whole and unsullied.

The same is true of those who minister the Word. Some, we know, are mere rogues. Some are flatterers who, so to speak, put God's Word up for sale. Others are mercenaries who preach only for profit; others still are full of pride and ambition and are eager to show off. Still others are depraved or immoral, drunkards and such. For all that, God's Word must be held in reverence among us, and the name 'pastor' honoured as holy, since it is founded in God; it does not depend on the fickleness of men and on their propensity for evil.[23] That, to put it briefly, is what we have to learn. The rest we will explain at another time.

Now let us cast ourselves down before the face of our good God, acknowledging our sins, beseeching him so to cleanse us by his Holy Spirit that, vile and impure though we are, he may remake us as living stones in his temple. And may we be truly built on the foundation he has laid, which is Jesus Christ our Lord. And though we are but poor teachers whose voice is barely heard, may we be touched by God's thunder which resounds in every place, and may we be continually transformed after the pattern of his righteousness. And since we see so many infirmities within us, let us persevere to the end in prayer, being strengthened in the unity of the faith, and not departing from its purity whatever troubles and impediments the devil puts in our way. May we overcome every difficulty that lies before us, and run the race we have begun until at last we reach our appointed goal. Therefore together let us say, Almighty God, our heavenly Father . . .

2

THE BROKEN BLESSED

*So Jesus, seeing the crowd, went up into a mountain; and when he
was seated, his disciples drew near to him. ² And opening his
mouth he taught them, saying, ³ Blessed are the poor in spirit, for
the kingdom of heaven is theirs. ⁴ Blessed are those who grieve, for
they will be comforted* (Matt. 5:1–4).

*Then lifting up his eyes upon his disciples, he said, Blessed are you
poor, for the kingdom of God is yours. ²¹ Blessed are you who now
are hungry, for you will be filled* (Luke 6:20–21).

*T*here is no doubt that from time to time the Gospel writers
chose to set down what might be called a summary of our
Lord Jesus Christ's teaching. They were not concerned to record
every word, but were content to briefly reveal how our Lord established his little church from the beginning and the instruction he
gave to his disciples.

In this passage we read that, having withdrawn into the mountain, and looking at the disciples, he taught them where man's true
blessedness is to be found. As for St Matthew's expression, *He
opened his mouth,* this is a Hebrew turn of phrase. True, the Gospel
writers did not write in Hebrew, as can be readily seen. They all
wrote in Greek, but nevertheless preserved the character of their
native tongue. This is something we observe among every nation.
Unless a Frenchman or a German has a thorough grounding in

Latin, he will always retain features of the language he learned as a child. That was God's intention here, to convince us that what was written was not the work of outsiders, but of men who had been born and bred in the country – rough, uneducated men who knew only their own language and what their mothers or nurses had taught them. In other words, they had not been to some advanced school in order to acquire superior learning.[1]

Here, then, we have an introduction, signifying that Jesus began to explain to his disciples matters which were most useful to them and which were to be carefully remembered and obeyed. His aim is to show where true peace of mind lies, and what goals are especially worth pursuing. This was a topic constantly debated by the pagans of old. The principal question posed by the philosophers was the nature and purpose of the sovereign good (for that was the term they used). We might call it by another name – man's true blessedness. There is of course no one who does not desire to be blessed. Indeed, if the dumb creatures were able to speak, and were capable of this kind of blessedness, they too would say, 'Yes, to be blessed is better than anything else.' And they would make that their goal. Man, therefore, who, on the one hand, feels his wretchedness and is distressed by it, and who, on the other, is able to discriminate, knowing where the true good lies, makes blessedness his aim, so far as he is able.

Among the pagan philosophers, the more worldly minded maintained simply that we are blessed when we are free of pain; others, when we are able to satisfy our appetite for pleasure; still others made virtue alone the source of blessedness. This last opinion was expressed in a much more sophisticated way. The word 'virtue' will always be held in esteem: though virtue itself may be in short supply, the vilest of men would blush to think they did not value this most admirable quality. Certain philosophers have argued along more subtle lines, claiming that virtue, in and of itself, cannot make us happy, and that the happy man is the one who always behaves properly. It is, they say, only when virtue is nurtured by contentment that we attain supreme happiness.[2] Now when all sides have had their say and argued back and forth, it is absolutely true that inner peace is what we all crave. We are so obsessed with the idea that we naturally regard as unhappy anyone who suffers poverty, want or sickness, who limps miserably through life, who never has a day's good health or who endures calumny or disgrace. Such things, we feel, are quite contrary to our nature. Never, as long as we possess reason and common sense, will we concede that someone could be happy who is beaten, physically abused and scorned, who is robbed of his goods and who spends every waking hour sighing and moaning. In short, we cannot reconcile the blessedness we seek with the idea of shame, poverty, hunger, thirst and other such afflictions.

Here we need to reflect on the kind of life to which our Lord Jesus Christ calls us once we are in his school. He bids each of us renounce self, and take up our cross. The word 'cross' implies that everyone should carry with him his own gallows, that we should be like those poor wretches who have a knife to their throat, that we should be afflicted and mocked, that not only should death be our companion but that we should be vilified and slandered as well, insulted and spat upon. We are meant to endure all of that, to bear it bravely like a burden placed upon our shoulders, just as a traveller might carry his bundle on his back. And so our Lord declares that we cannot come after him or be counted as one of his followers unless we take up our load. To do that we have to give up our comforts! We are to be as men condemned, under threat of death, beset from every side, our life lived in continual weakness.

In a word, to take up our load is to be reckoned as utterly miserable so far as this world is concerned. That is the plain ABC which is taught in the school of our Lord Jesus Christ.[3]

What if we were to cling to the idea – so firmly planted in our heads that we seem to have been born with it – that if we suffer affliction in the world we can never really be blessed? If that were the case, which of us would not run a mile from the Lord Jesus Christ or willingly consent to be his disciple, even supposing we accepted his teaching and hailed him as God's Son who calls us to himself? In that case we might well say, 'Yes, but surely he knows our weakness and frailty? Why should he not put up with us as we are?' Each one of us would take our shoulder from the wheel if we truly held the idea – deeply rooted, as I said – that blessedness is only for those who are comfortable and at ease.

That is why our Lord preached as he does here to his disciples, demonstrating that our happiness and blessedness do not come from the world's applause, or from the enjoyment of wealth, honours, gratification and pleasure. On the contrary, we may be utterly oppressed, in tears and weeping, persecuted and to all appearances ruined: none of that affects our standing or diminishes our happiness. Why? Because we have in view the ultimate outcome. That is what Christ would have us remember, so as to correct the false ideas we feed upon and which so muddle our thinking that we cannot accept his yoke. He reminds us that we must look further ahead and consider the outcome of our afflictions, our tears, the persecutions we suffer and the insults we bear. When once we see how God turns all of that to good and to our salvation, we may conclude that blessing will assuredly be ours, however contrary such things are to our nature.

Our Lord begins with *the poor in spirit*. Some commentators have tried to explain this phrase too cleverly, assuming that the spiritually poor are those who have no confidence in themselves, but recognize that they are without integrity, wisdom, and righteousness. Such an interpretation is, to be sure, good and wholesome; it does not, however, fit the context.[4] St Luke makes no mention of 'spirit': he refers only to *the poor*. In fact Hebrew uses the same word to describe both a man of lowly rank, and one who has suffered humiliation and loss. This is because prosperity puffs us up with pride and ambition: as a result we long for the limelight, and are keen to get the better of our neighbour. On the other hand, once God takes the rod to us and tames us, our haughty manners disappear.

In so far, then, as suffering disciplines us, Jesus' expression designates both the poor and the humble. The same is true of the body. If a man is physically strong, in the prime of life and untouched by illness, he exults, free to leap about as he chooses. There is no holding him. But after two or three months' sickness he drags his feet, he is a different man. Whereas before he was totally reckless, given to excess of every kind and able to cope with anything, now he can scarcely manage to chew a morsel and swallow it. Before he would run here and there; now he cannot even rise from his bed.

What is true of the body, is true also of the soul. When we get everything we want, our appetites inevitably know no bounds. They are like the waves which foam on the sea: nothing can hold them back. So when we are puffed up with pride, we are like drunken men who have forgotten what temperance is. When, on the other hand, God brings us into contempt in the eyes of men, and when everyone has had a laugh at our expense, when our good name is slandered and we are the butt of hatred, envy, and spite, when false charges and slanders are brought against us, when we are poor and cast adrift without comfort or aid – when, in short, we have experienced everything we call adversity, then we learn the meaning of restraint, and hang our heads which once we held too high. Since, however, many contrive to pander to their pride, however much God may buffet them and encourage them to humility – since, I say, there are many who are almost unteachable, that is why our Lord felt it necessary to add the words *in spirit*. His meaning is that those who are poor are blessed, in so far as poverty has disciplined them, producing in them poverty of spirit. That is, their heart is no longer proud or set on evil, as is the case with many.

There are many indeed who chafe at the bit. Think of the wild animals who, when they are chained up or are held in an iron cage, are as aggressive as ever. We keep bears, wolves, and lions in captivity, but they remain as they have always been. So it is with men. Although the Lord Jesus Christ keeps them on a tight rein, still they fume and grind their teeth, and their pride bursts forth worse than before. So God, for his part, has to bear down hard on them so as to expel the poison which otherwise might kill them. Not that they improve as a result. They grow even worse, rant and rage and flaunt their devilish fury in the face of God. That, I repeat, is how it is with many people.

Does this mean, then, that their poverty, their experience of adversity, serves no purpose? Not at all! It makes their guilt all the worse when they appear before the bar of God. They are examples to us all. The great of this world are highly esteemed; they enjoy men's praise, they have everything their heart might wish for: wealth, a well-stocked table, every good thing. It is not, then, surprising if such as these forget themselves, become drunk on creature comforts and glory in their empty pride. But supposing a man suffers adversity: everyone resents and slanders him, he languishes in this world like a man half-dead. Yet if for all that he still felt pleasure and pride in himself, and remained stiff-necked and unyielding, would he not be going against nature?

The fact is that it is not simply a matter of being poor or miserable. There are many who experience poverty without being humbled by it. Rather they resist God as much as they can. So we must learn that poverty, as our Lord understands the term, must enter within, purging us from all pride and presumption. We must recognize that we are nothing. That person, then, is truly blessed, who is poor in his own estimation, who willingly abases himself, who sees nothing good in himself, makes no false claims about himself, and instead accepts rejection by the world. Here we see the real significance of Jesus' words, and the benefit which we may gain from them.

Someone may ask whether the converse is true: are those who are rich in spirit under God's curse? That, I am sure, is what our Lord means to convey. True, he will go on to pronounce a blessing on those who are persecuted – which is not to say that everyone must be persecuted, otherwise we would be like the hypocrites who relish such things! No, when he says, *Blessed are the persecuted,* he means that we should not shun persecution when God chooses to do battle with us or when we are unjustly afflicted: we should bear everything with patience.

So far as our text here is concerned, Jesus Christ clearly intends to contrast the rich in spirit – that is, those who foolishly pride themselves on their prosperity – with the poor in spirit – those who, rightly humbled by the experience of affliction, have put aside pride and look to God alone for help. This, then, is what we may glean from this passage: all who are rich in spirit, who are wrapped in self-esteem, who love earthly pleasures and social recognition, who claim merit on the grounds of birth or property, prestige or reputation – all such are accursed and rejected by Christ, as Scripture affirms in a passage to which we will later come.[5] That is the lesson we must attend to here.

We have already seen the reason for this in the song of the Virgin Mary, when she says that *God pulls down the mighty and the kings from their seats, and lifts up the lowly and the once despised.*[6] If that was all she had said, we might well have objected, 'What? Does God enjoy changing things around, playing cat-and-mouse games with people, tossing them about like a ball, or treating them like counters which are worth whatever you like – 20 shillings one time, 100 another, 1,000 after that, only to be worth, on the last throw, no more than a penny?'[7] If God made sport of us like that, we would indeed think it was absurd. For that reason the Virgin Mary adds, *God satisfies the hungry, but the well fed he sends away empty*. Here, then, she reveals why God effects such changes in the world.

Imagine a man who has enough not only to feed himself, but to live in pleasant and ostentatious style, and who is admired and fêted by all. How hard it would be for him not to gloat, like any great man carried away by ambition. His arrogance would be like that of the drunkard or of the glutton filled to bursting point: when their belly is stuffed with bread, wine, and food, they are so bloated they can scarcely turn around. So the Virgin Mary declares that people who thus misuse God's generous gifts will indeed have their fill, but will be sent away empty, and will learn what it is to be bloated only with wind. The hungry, on the other hand, God will fully satisfy.

The word 'hungry' has the same meaning as the expression 'humble in spirit'. Of course there are people who are hungry but who have no appetite for food. But when a poor man knows what it is he lacks, and turns to the one who can supply his need, and in all humility asks for help, that man is truly 'poor in spirit'. Therefore, when affliction makes us poor in spirit, when, that is, necessity compels us to look to God for help, that is when we find true blessedness.

A similar meaning attaches to our Lord's next remark, that *the kingdom of heaven belongs to the poor in spirit*. By this we are to understand that we should not be content with what our eyes see, but that we should have in view the final goal. When those philosophers who valued virtue above all else sought to prove that affliction did not make men miserable, they had to invent a man of steel, an anvil, so to speak, on which the hammer could make no impression. Ultimately, of course, that was mere fantasy, pure folly on their part. Even supposing men were found who could put on a brave show in public, and pass for valiant and steadfast individuals, the fact is that inwardly they seethed because they were rebels against God. They reasoned from first principles: 'I am indeed a mortal man. I must bear all things with patience. I have no choice, I must comply.' (They take necessity, you see, as their guiding rule.) 'What would be the point of resisting? I must accept what I cannot avoid.' That, I say, is what they call patience: it is nothing but a form of anger, since they are in rebellion against God. Their steadfastness is really a wilful act of refusal. They would have been happy to retreat if they had been able to; but they had no other choice than to weakly yield, since they believed it is blind fate which governs everything. What their philosophy taught was so much nonsense.

Our Lord Jesus Christ, by contrast, does not lead us off into speculative byways which have no practical effect. He sets us on a firm foundation, so that, as long as we rest upon it, we will not be moved. And however many storms and winds arise, and however much heaven and earth are mixed and muddled, our happiness is always secure as long as we look to the kingdom of heaven.

So this is what the passage teaches: in order to taste the blessedness of which God's Son speaks, we must learn first that this world is a pathway to something else; it is not a place where we are to rest or where real life is to be found; we must press further on and lift up our eyes to the heavenly inheritance. Thus, all who are tied to this world, who rely on men's accepted wisdom and who look for happiness only in earthly pleasures, cannot possibly grasp the importance of this teaching. Instead, it will be a constant annoyance to them.

What of those who are believers? They will certainly experience painful battles within, whenever they ask themselves: 'How can I be blessed and yet condemn myself to so much misery?' For that is what poverty in spirit is all about: it means that a person is close to despair, and that he is near to ruin until God comes to his rescue. This, to be sure, is a matter of much controversy. For it seems wrong that we should be blessed and at the same time in distress, that we should be bitter and groan inwardly, not knowing where to turn, to the point that we finally confess, 'Alas! If God does not take pity on us, we are finished!' So having, in our worldly wisdom, run here and there, we are forced back to this conclusion: 'Woe to us if we are poor, hungry and persecuted.'

But when we remember that God has placed us in the world in order to test our obedience, that we are only passing through, that there is no place here to stop or rest, but that we have an inheritance prepared for us in heaven – once we are seized by that thought, blessedness is no longer for us a hidden secret. That, too, is what St Paul teaches, when he affirms that believers should glory in their sufferings, since (as he says) affliction produces hope, and the experience of God's mercy to his people strengthens our hope, so that we are never put to shame. The point he goes on to make is exactly what I have been saying, that is, that the promise has been given to us, and that if our salvation lies in hope, it must at present remain hidden. We do not hope for something we can see.[8] No-one would say, 'I hope that supper will soon be ready', when the table is actually set and the food placed on it. We hope instead for something of which we are still not sure. It is the same with our salvation. We can indeed have unshakeable certainty concerning God's truth. But here it is a question of how we perceive and apprehend things.

The goal then is necessarily uncertain to us; we must recognize that we are a long way off, and incapable of understanding. If, then, our salvation lies in hope, it is hidden; and if it is hidden, we must count ourselves blessed not in terms of what we see or of what we now possess. We count ourselves blessed because we groan here below, and wait for God to call us to himself and for Jesus Christ to welcome us, he who is our life and the source of everything good.

How, then, may we profitably apply all this to ourselves? By learning how to meditate on the promises of everlasting salvation contained in the Word of God. Those promises separate us from the world. It is as if God were holding his hand out to us, and saying, 'Poor creatures, there you are sunk deep in the mire. When you follow your own desires, when amusement is all you can think of, you imagine your happiness is complete. All that is but a passing shadow. Do not be deceived: see where your true welfare lies, and set your sights on me.'

God's promises are most useful, then, in detaching us from the world. And when we have finally left present things behind, then we will know that poverty, affliction, distress, trouble, and everything else which would destroy us, cannot touch us. It is enough that God loves us, that his love has been made known to us, and that by faith we lay hold of that love when we leave this world. Let us go on, then, to finish our course, until in due time God confirms his promises to us.

It is indeed true that in this world God spares us so that we are able to taste something of his goodness and have cause to rejoice. But joy does not last; we can never expect real satisfaction from it. It cannot be said too often that although God has pity on our infirmities, and so treats us less severely than he ought, giving us nourishment, more even than nature requires – even so, mixed in with this is so much affliction and distress that we will always lament our lot, saying: 'Poor wretch that I am!', until such time as we have learnt to go straight to him.

Moreover, much the same thing is said in the phrase which follows. These are not different themes, and it is good for us that they are repeated. It is as if the idea had been chewed over for us so that we could get it down more easily. As our own experience suggests, this line of teaching is rather difficult to digest.[9] That, then, is why Jesus says *blessed are those who weep, for in the end they will rejoice and be comforted*. Here he affirms more or less what we have already learnt. For if we are poor in spirit, we cannot avoid weeping; we cannot be other than distressed. We are not, after all, without feelings, like those madmen I mentioned earlier, who expect us to remain as immovable as an anvil or a rock! Such a thing goes against our nature. We have instead to feel our miseries, which are meant to press us to the point where we bend and break: we can no longer hold our heads up, our breath is taken from us, we are, so to speak, dead men.[10]

That is why our Lord in this passage associates weeping and poverty in spirit. It is as if he were saying: 'When I tell you that nothing will take away your blessedness, however oppressed and afflicted you are, I do not mean that you should dumbly resist regardless of feelings, or that you should be like senseless blocks of wood. No! You will weep, you will experience want, dishonour, illness, and other kinds of affliction in this world. These things you will suffer; they will wound you to the very core and make you weep. But nothing will take your blessedness from you. Why? Because my last word to you is: Wait for the consolation from on high.'

So then, it is nowhere said that when we weep we will be blessed because of our virtue, or that we will shed tears because tyrants and evil-doers are oppressing us.[11] Nor are we meant to be wholly self-absorbed: there is precious little happiness within, for we would always be miserable when we took account of all that is inside of us. When, however, we remember that God has promised to comfort us, provided we seek him with tears and in humility, and patiently obey his will, then we need not doubt that our very afflictions will appear a salutary trial – spurs, so to speak, which urge us on to do our duty. When we have learnt that, our blessedness will be assured. And why? Because we look for it, not in ourselves, but in God.

Here we see just how different our Lord's teaching is from what we read in the books and writings of the pagans, whatever wisdom they may have had in their own time. Their thoughts, however deep and persuasive, were no more than smoke and deception. By contrast, what Jesus Christ teaches stands firm and never passes away. We must, therefore, turn our backs both on ourselves and on the world, and seek from God the things we cannot find on earth. That is the point we need to grasp. True, there are many about us who shed tears, but their tears are like the howls of brute beasts, as when a bull bellows or an ox cries as it is slaughtered. That, I say, is how it is with many.

What I mean is that when unbelievers weep, the tears they shed are less than real. They lament, sure enough, and repeatedly cry, 'Alas! Alas!', but, as I have said, they do no more than howl. What we must do is learn to weep before our God. It is to him that our tears must send us. When we do that, we will experience the truth of David's words, 'Lord, you have put my tears in a bottle.'[12] Just as someone looks after a precious perfume or a costly ointment, so, David says, God stores up our tears. Of course, tears fall to the ground, or else we wipe them away with our hand. Nevertheless, when we weep before God, not one tear will be lost: God will carefully preserve them all.

We are thus brought back to the theme of consolation of which this passage speaks. We see that both verses convey the same message, which is that, as disciples of Jesus Christ, we bear our cross and carry our gallows with us, like souls condemned to die, mocked, insulted and slandered; yet nothing can ever rob us of our blessedness or take away our reason for rejoicing.

If we turn briefly to St Luke, we note that, whereas St Matthew says, *Blessed are the poor in spirit, and those who weep,* St Luke says, *Blessed are you who weep, and blessed are you who are poor.* Our Lord means us not only to understand his teaching in a collective sense, but to receive it as a word spoken to each of us individually, and to be personally appropriated.

Having sounded our hearts, he wants to show us precisely why he has chosen to prepare us in this way. It is for each of us to apply our Lord's teaching. He wishes us to know that when he speaks, he is talking intimately to each of us.

This is what he says: 'To be poor, you must be poor in spirit, truly humbled; you must become as nothing in your inmost self. When that is done, the world may judge you as wretched, and you may judge yourself the same way. But when I offer you blessedness, you will be able to reply with a bold 'Amen', and you will receive that blessedness. In the end you will know that you have not been deceived, but that you have attained your inheritance. Then you will understand how God, who brings sorrow upon his children while they are in the world, will in the next give them gladness. Those whom he once kept hungry, he will plentifully feed.'

Now let us cast ourselves down before the face of our good God, acknowledging our sins, praying that he might take away all our earthly desires, that we might learn not to seek the corruptible things of this world nor look for our happiness in them. And let us not be so drunk on Satan's pleasures and seductions that we stray from the path of true and lasting blessedness, to which God calls and invites us. But when we find ourselves overwhelmed by troubles and distress, let us learn to look to him whatever the circumstance, and to find in him all our joy and glory. Therefore together let us say, Almighty God, our heavenly Father . . .

3

MEEKNESS AND MERCY

christ want on to say

Blessed are the meek, for they will inherit the earth. ⁶Blessed are those who hunger and thirst on account of righteousness, for they will be filled. ⁷ Blessed are the merciful, for mercy will be shown them (Matt. 5:5–7).

Then lifting up his eyes upon his disciples, he said, Blessed are you who are poor, for the kingdom of God is yours. ²¹ᵃ Blessed are you who hunger now, for you will be filled (Luke 6:20–21a) .

*I*f we would only heed what nature teaches us we would enjoy the happiest state that humans could desire. For God has created all of us in his own image, so that we have only to look at our neighbour to see ourselves. We are one flesh. And although appearances and attitudes are very different, it is impossible to efface the unity which God has conferred on us. If only that were firmly etched in our minds, we would all be living at peace with each other, in a kind of earthly paradise.

The opposite, however, is the case. Everyone around us follows his own interests and looks to his own advantage; everyone wants to lord it over others. Hence our pride, our surliness, our venom the instant we are provoked. Harshness and even cruelty abound. We are vindictive and cause no end of trouble: it is as if lightning should fall from heaven every time someone is offended. So if in the course of life we endure many difficulties, we do not have to look far for the explanation: the pain men suffer comes from their fellow men. It is, of course, true that people all have their excuses. They want nothing better, they say, than to be gentle and mild-mannered, and to show patience toward those among whom they live. But, they add, it is not possible to deny our human nature: we must hunt with the hounds, because to be a sheep is to risk becoming someone else's dinner.[1] That, then, is the excuse usually offered by men to cloak their actions. In reality so full are they of bitterness, arrogance, and pride that they cannot abide one another. It is all the more fitting, then, that we remember the lesson which the Son of God has for us here. For although we think we are hard done by when we cannot retaliate against those who ill-treat us, he tells us that *it is the peace-makers and the meek who will possess the earth.*

Now common sense tells us such a thing is not credible. Experience, too, suggests that victory and success go to the boldest and most aggressive, while the unassuming dare not open their mouths to protest or complain, even though others may rob and fleece them of all they have. So common sense dictates that people who are meek will always suffer insult and abuse, unable even to find some small corner where they can draw breath or shake off their pursuers – lambs, so to speak, among a pack of wolves. For all that, our Lord Jesus Christ made no false claim when he promised that *the meek will inherit the earth.*

This teaching might make no sense to the worldly-wise; but believers have tasted enough of its truth to know that these are not empty words. For however much men may rage and continually fight, attack, steal, and commit other acts of violence, however much, I say, men may struggle to come out on top, if we candidly consider their real state of mind, we will find that the opposite is true. Everyone of necessity is their enemy. Naturally, if they manage to acquire the power of tyrants, no one will openly dare oppose them. Even so they will inwardly fret and fume; they know that they are friendless, and in their anxiety and agitation they distrust everybody. Blind suspicion, like a thorn-prick, drives them on, or like a sharp spike blinds their vision, filling them with panic and scattering them like lost souls who wrongly imagine that an enemy is after them.

And even supposing they had nothing to fear from other men, God would certainly show himself to be their judge. Just as they unsettle heaven and earth by their reckless action, so God unsettles them within: their conscience, as Isaiah says, will be like the storm-tossed waves of the sea. They will be at war with themselves, in a fine old state. They will never be at rest, as the prophet himself declares.[2] That is why the law explicitly says that the life of such men hangs by a thread, that their eyes will be sunk in their fore-heads, that their limbs will tremble and, when morning comes, they will cry: 'Will I live long enough to see night fall?' And when it is evening, they will ask: 'Will I manage to last through the night? Supposing I were attacked, what could I do?'[3]

Only those blinded by vanity, lies, and prejudice will fail to see how true Isaiah's prophecy is. We all know how it is with those who prey like wolves upon their fellow-men, who rob and devour and who, out of arrogance and pride, try to gain all they can. They never know a moment's peace. They may own the earth, they may be mighty lords, yet, wherever they tread, they are like dead men. For all their castles and fortresses and well-armed guards, the fact remains they are in prison. In the open field and with a numerous escort, they are insecure, in a constant state of fear and trembling.

In short, wherever they go, they see all too well that they are like Cain, without peace of mind and beset on all sides with anxiety. In possessing much they finally possess nothing, since they are in-capable of enjoying what they think they have. That is how it is with all whom this world counts as great. Inwardly they are in a state of turmoil, although in men's estimation they have no cause to be. Why, then, are they like this? It is because God brings trouble on those who bring trouble on everyone else. They are at their wits' end, seeing enemies all around them and judging every man, both great and small, to be a threat. For although no one dares say a word or lifts a finger against them, they are greatly resented. The whole world may be mute and honours may be heaped upon them: God will nevertheless stretch out his hand to punish them as they deserve.

Conversely, the poor, who walk in sincerity and who patiently persevere, are secure; however many cruelties and trials they suffer, they are sure to inherit the earth, as Psalm 37 says.[4] Although they may not own one foot of ground, nor meadow, vineyard, field, or house, they are persuaded that it is God who has placed them in this world; and although they may be like birds perched on a branch, they nevertheless can say with quiet assurance: 'God will direct my steps wherever I am. The earth too will welcome and nourish me for it was created for that end. God will allow me to find a home here, and he will care for me as his guest as long as it pleases him.'

When a person has that assurance, when he knows that God upholds and will continue to uphold him, he is infinitely richer than those who clutch and claw their way through life, and who in their haste to swallow everything are satisfied neither with kingdoms, duchies, countries, or towns. When their work is done, however, they have nowhere they can retreat to, no hiding-place, no refuge, for God is against them and every man is their enemy. Although believers are strangers and wanderers in this world, is not the home they have on earth much better than any earthly dominion, the source of so much torment to all who covet it?

Experience also teaches believers that God is watching over them. Imagine what would happen if it were otherwise. Think for a moment of the malevolence and fury of the unbelievers: they are the mirror-image of Satan their father! The world would be full of murderers, and all good, peace-loving people would soon be swept away, if God did not use his secret powers to keep them safe. That, I say, is what we can expect if we wilfully shut our eyes to the grace of God so clearly revealed in this passage.

What is more, we know that God has given us the Lord Jesus Christ to be our Shepherd. As such, his most vital work is to preserve our souls until we attain the eternal salvation which he has won for us. Nevertheless, even in this transitory life, he cares also for our physical being. Let us therefore be his sheep, for he is not a shepherd to wolves. If we choose to live like wild beasts, throw off all restraint, and contrive – as the saying goes – to add insult to injury, and if, as soon as we are offended or upset, we take up arms to avenge ourselves and try to create as much havoc as we can, we cannot expect Jesus to be our Shepherd. What he requires is that we hear his voice. Sheep and lambs hear their master's voice: let them be our example! If, then, we are honest and sincere, we will surely discover how strong a protector the Son of God is, for he will employ his Father's power to keep and sustain us.

The meek will inherit the earth. That is a notion which the human mind cannot entertain. Instead, it is commonly said that all who are gracious, sincere and long-suffering are poor fools; they would do better retaliating than allowing their good nature to be abused. Nevertheless, what Jesus elsewhere declares is true: the best and most preferable course is to maintain our sincerity, to practise patient endurance when we are maligned, not to render evil for evil but to overcome evil with good.[5] If we do that, we will have found the one true way by which we may possess the earth. What, after all, do the bold and brutal seek, when men tremble to see them and dread their coming? Is not their aim to possess the earth, to rule it as a tyrant? Yes, that is what they covet for themselves.

But, as we have seen, they themselves are captive in every place on earth. In open fields, towns, castles, and fortresses – everyone is their enemy; they are at war with themselves; God pursues them wherever they may be.

As for us, we must constantly return to what God's Son declares to us, for what he says is eternally true and trustworthy. Let us be clear about this: provided, as he says, we exercise self-control and are patient, provided we possess that gentleness which he requires of us and to which he calls us, we will inherit the whole earth. With thankful, free and open hearts we will enjoy the good things which God in his kindness provides for us here. We are assured too that we will always be at peace, whatever troubles we are in.

That said, we should recognize that this promise is not yet totally fulfilled. It is enough that today we experience its truth in part. Scripture rightly says that the last day is the day of our redemption, the day on which God's children will be revived and restored.[6] So we must patiently wait to possess the inheritance which Christ has promised, and to claim the earth as his gift to us. We should be content to pursue our course to the end and complete our earthly pilgrimage. Regardless of where we are, regardless of the trials we bear and the oppression and losses we endure, we should, I say, be content to trust God's assurance, and the testimony of our conscience, that all will be ours because we are his children and heirs. Furthermore, we should stop envying the proud, the violent, and the domineering who think they have everything when, like brute beasts, they have come out on top. That in essence is what this verse teaches us. We should therefore hate the devilish proverb which urges us to 'run with the hare and hunt with the hounds'. Instead we should place our Lord's protection above the impulse to retaliate or defend our cause. For his power to sustain us is unlimited, and he will prove immeasurably stronger than any foe. That, then, is what we have to grasp here.

Next, Scripture says, *Blessed are those who hunger and thirst for righteousness' sake, for they will be filled.* St Luke says simply, *Blessed are you who hunger now, for you will be filled.* St Matthew adds the word 'righteousness' for the sake of precision. Even so he has been misinterpreted. Some have looked for a meaning higher and more subtle than is justified. We must be zealous, they say, for righteousness – that is, we must yearn for a more just and upright order, so that when God sees how earnest we are, he will change the world for the better and so gladden our hearts.

Now that is a perfectly good thing to teach in the proper context. The Gospel writers, however, fully and faithfully explain Christ's meaning here. From St Luke's words no such subtle or deep meaning can be derived.[7] He does not say that we are to hunger for righteousness or that, in the face of so much evil, we should cry to God, begging him to set the world to rights. So when Scripture says, *Blessed are those who hunger*, it means the same as we saw before: blessed are those who mourn, who are poor in spirit and therefore distressed, and who turn to God for refuge and relief.

Why, then, does St Matthew add the word 'righteousness'? To express a perfectly appropriate idea. What he really means is that God's children will not only hunger and thirst – that is, suffer oppression, bereft of help and comfort – but that they will have right on their side, since they will not have given anyone cause to harm them. Not that they seek special privileges or favours for having injured no one. They do not try to win their case by underhand means. All they ask is that they be treated equitably and not harassed without cause. They have every right to feel this way, but their wish will not be easily or immediately granted. How wretched and unhappy they would be, were it not for the promise given here, that *they will be filled.*[8]

That is how our Lord's words here are best understood. He first of all warns us that we will not enjoy a state of rest or repose, but that, on the contrary, we will hunger and thirst, and that our wish for all of life's necessities will be disappointed. We will not always find food and drink when we need them; or, if we are fed, we may be short of clothing or shelter. In the second place, he says that we will be sorely afflicted, that there will be no one to help whichever way we turn. It will be as if people might spit in our faces with perfect impunity!

That is a hard and bitter condition to endure, especially when we think of our own infirmities. For we are so frail that the merest nothing fills us with despair. Let us learn, therefore, to rest in the certain hope that we will finally be filled, and that God will supply everything we lack. If today we are like those who are at death's door, devoid of inner strength and outside help, if today we are in the direst of straits, let this hope support and sustain us, as we look to God whose work is to satisfy the hungry.

Is it surprising if, when we are in the right and when we seek no special advantage for ourselves, we should nevertheless experience hunger? We may indeed be innocent of aggression, anxious not to profit at someone else's expense and asking only justice and equity for ourselves: we are meant nevertheless to endure hunger and thirst. God will leave us to languish for a time in order to test our patience or our faith. For if today we were perfectly at ease, lacking nothing, surrounded by people eager to please and with no one to trouble or upset us, what would be the point of urging us to practise what is taught here?

To hunger and thirst is therefore, for us, a necessity. And since, as we have seen, we are to be meek, as men living among wild beasts whose teeth are sharp and whose claws are ready to tear, rend, and destroy us, we must press on in patience and sincerity. We should be hungry and thirsty for prayer to God. And although he allows us to suffer affliction even when we are in the right, we should not give way to sadness, despair, or blind panic. We should hold firm to the expectation that, in the end, he will provide for all our needs. That is something else our text has to teach us.

Our Lord Jesus Christ goes on to add, *Blessed are the merciful, for they will obtain mercy*. Here again is a saying which is quite foreign to our normal way of thinking. Where else do we imagine happiness to lie, except in the absence of worry or distress? 'Leave us alone', we cry. 'Let others suffer in silence. We don't want to know. We don't wish to be bothered.' Peace of mind, indifference to anything else – it is enough if we are able to satisfy our physical wants and contemplate all earth's villainies without feeling sorrow, disquiet, or distress.

That is why many imagine they are blessed when they are at ease, able to live the good life without thinking of what is happening around them. They want only to block their ears so as to shut out news which might affect them. For there are two kinds of emotions which disturb us: unhappiness which arises from personal misfortune, and compassion when we see some poor person suffering beyond measure – someone, perhaps, who is unjustly oppressed, or who has lost all his worldly goods, unhappy orphans without fathers, wives without husbands, or unexpected events which, I repeat, greatly trouble us. Those who are looking for happiness (as they understand the term), seek to escape personal misfortune in the form of injury to themselves or loss of property. They love men's approval; they revel in entertainment, in laughter, in good fortune; they want flattery and praise. That is one point to consider.

But there is more. Supposing they are told, 'Do you see that poor wretch? He's suffering terribly. He has nothing – no money – and his health has gone. It's pitiful to behold.' News like that is a source of annoyance to worldly people. They, as we well know, will deliberately harden their hearts, and will not only not feel pity for the miseries which others endure, but will be perfectly content for everyone to go hungry. They may own large stocks of wheat, but the world's population can perish for all they care, providing their own wallets are filled. It doesn't matter to them if poor folk starve, as long as business is going well.

There are many more examples of this kind. All of them show how easy it is for men who scorn God to cast aside all pity and compassion, in order to avoid worry and trouble. Now Scripture says something very different here. We must patiently bear our own afflictions – a point we have already noted – but we must also bear the afflictions of our neighbour. We must assume their identity, as it were, so as to be deeply touched by their suffering and moved by love to mourn with them. We must weep with those who weep, as St Paul exhorts us to do.[9]

We said earlier that although we are exposed to misfortune, trouble, oppression, and abuse, we can be truly happy because God blesses our sufferings when we look to him. In this verse, the Lord Jesus Christ takes believers one step further, teaching that as well as being meek and patient when we are afflicted, we must be at one with others in their distress, and so touched with compassion for their suffering as to look for ways of helping them, as if their pain were ours. I say again, since God has brought us together in order to make of us one body, all members are necessarily one, and each individual must take his share of suffering, in order to relieve those who can bear no more. That is the truth we must grasp here.

What is pity? Briefly put, it is nothing else but the pain we feel at someone else's sorrow. A man may be healthy and content, with plenty to eat and drink, and safe from any threat of danger. When, however, he sees his neighbour in distress, he is bound to feel for him, to share his sorrow, to shoulder some of his burden and so lighten the load. That is what mercy is. The same idea is conveyed in our language by the word 'alms'. Unfortunately, the meaning of 'alms' has been misconstrued. What people mean by 'alms-giving' is not something inspired by feelings of humanity. Of course one can give to a poor person, but it is like a ransom, a tribute, or exaction given grudgingly and with reluctance. There is no suggestion that when a rich man gives of his substance, he says to himself, 'Here is a member of Christ's body, we are all joined together.' It is all the more important, therefore, to understand that helping others amounts to nothing unless we are moved by a love which comes from the heart, and which bids us bear our share of the misfortune we see around us. And because God has bound us all together, no one can turn away and live only for himself. There is no room here for the indifference which promises tranquillity and the pleasures of a comfortable life: we must enlarge our affections as the law of love requires.

So when we see some who are sick or poor or destitute, and others who are in trouble and distress of body or mind, we should say, 'This person belongs to the same body as I do.' And then we should prove by our deeds that we are merciful. We can proclaim our pity for those who suffer time without number; but unless we actually assist them, our claims will be worthless. There are plenty of people who will say, 'Oh dear! How terrible to be like that poor man!' Yet they simply brush it all aside, making no attempt to help. Expressions of pity stir no one into action. In short, this world is full of mercy if words are to be believed; in reality it is all pretence. St James vigorously condemns this attitude in chapter 2 of his Epistle.[10] It is the height of insolence to say, 'Ah me, what a shame!', when no one is willing to lift a finger or even utter a word in order to help the distressed. We must learn, therefore, first to be kind and compassionate toward those who suffer; and then to make diligent use of the opportunities which God affords.

This verse has a promise attached to it, for we are notoriously slow to act. It is true also that what God's Son says here runs counter to our natural inclinations. We do not easily assent to it. The promise thus serves as a point of entry. For if the text simply said, *Blessed are the merciful,* we would reject it out of hand. When, however, Christ tells us that we are all in need of mercy, both from his heavenly Father and from our fellow men, and that we can only obtain it if we are merciful – that at least should prompt us to look more closely at ourselves. When we begin to savour the truth of what we are told here, we can only conclude that to be merciful is indeed part of the blessedness enjoyed by God's children. It is a simple fact that we all need mercy.

Take, for example, the person who has everything he could wish for in this world: many disappointments will nevertheless come his way. Even princes, kings, and mighty lords endure at one time or another terrible ordeals, suffering sometimes in body, sometimes in mind. Although they might seek to build secure nests for themselves high above the clouds, God shows that they are mortal after all. They are compelled to see themselves as mere men, frail creatures. If the mighty, who already have a kind of paradise to themselves, are in need of mercy, how much more are we?

If we thought carefully about these things, we would be moved to show pity every time we saw our neighbour suffering want or affliction. It might be objected that the world itself shows little pity to those who have had pity on others. Attend, first, to this point. God, we know, holds men's hearts in his hands. He turns them whichever way he wills. Even if evil and arrogance, mischief and spite abound, he lays upon men the burden of humanity.[11] So although the world may have scant regard – indeed, contempt – for works of mercy done to the needy, God will nevertheless overrule so that, when we are in distress, he will not deny us our reward – mercy to the merciful.

This, as we will later see, is what our Lord Jesus Christ himself teaches, when he says that each of us will receive according to the measure we have given.[12] St James, too, rightly declares that the person who has failed to show mercy will be judged without mercy.[13]

Consider now this second point. Supposing God allowed such ingratitude to prevail among men that all our efforts to help the poor appeared wasted. What then? One day we must come before the great Judge. His mercy is our only hope. Supposing the world were full of cruelty and our good works a waste of time. We would have no less need of God's mercy. There is nothing in St James more fearful, more terrible than the words, *judgment without mercy*. If we had to appear before God's judgment seat to receive strict justice, what would become of us? It would have been better if we had been still-born, or had entered the world as fleas or lice or frogs – the lowest forms of life!

Since, then, our welfare and salvation depend wholly on God's mercy, should we not rejoice in his promise of pity and compassion when we, who have shown pity to our neighbour, lay before him our burden of pain? Is not God moved to welcome us, to be merciful to us, though because of our dreadful sins he might well have cast us out? Since we have this promise, we would have to be mad, out of our minds, to ignore the claims of mercy. That is what we have to remember here. It is a fact, moreover, that God allows us to taste at least in part what the Son confirms to us, for he is the true witness who has come from the Father's side to declare his will (as we read in chapter 18 of St John's Gospel).[14]

Know then that when we have been merciful, we ourselves will receive mercy, even from men. And however evil and ungrateful they may be, God will press them so hard that when we are in need they will help us, though the idea of serving God and dispensing charity may be far from their minds. It will be with them as it was with the Egyptians who, although enemies of God's people, were nevertheless compelled to hand over to them the most precious things they possessed.[15]

In any case, we have higher things to think of. We must ultimately give an account of how we have lived: if we have been
merciful, we will find that God is merciful to us. Moreover, mercy
does not simply consist of compassion toward those I have been
describing – the thirsty, the hungry, the sick, the hurt, and the
oppressed. It requires us also to bear with the infirmities of those
who, in themselves, deserve to be spurned. Of course, here as elsewhere, we must observe the balance which we find in Scripture.
When we show mercy to those who have erred, we must never
indulge them by outright flattery, nor ignore their wrongdoing so
that it grows even worse. We should show pity when we see that
our neighbours are still subject to many weaknesses, and we should
be patient with them, not in order to imitate them but to rebuke
their faults with kindness. We should never gloat as many do who
laugh and smirk over someone else's misfortune. Instead, we
should mourn and say, 'How sad, that poor man has given offence
to God.' It should distress us to see someone perishing who has
been so dearly redeemed by Christ's precious blood;[16] it should
distress us to see God's righteousness transgressed and his glory
diminished.

Believe me, such things should awaken our compassion. That is
how we will find mercy in God's sight – by having pity on those who
have gone astray or who have stumbled through weakness; by bearing with them and trying to set them back on their feet. St Paul
exhorts us to do both things: we are to exercise mercy without bias,
being careful not to indulge the fallen; conversely we are not to be so
harsh and extreme that we fail to support them. He tells us to rebuke
those who have gone astray, but with meekness of spirit. Reflect, he
says, that you too can sin; if you understand your own weakness, you
will have pity on those who are sinners like you.[17] In this way, then,
we see how, in every time and every place, we are to exercise kindness: by having compassion on those who have done wrong, by

helping those in need, by assisting those who are unjustly oppressed and by defending their cause, even though as a consequence wicked men may rise up in fury against us.

Concerning these things, note what is written in St Luke. *You yourselves are blessed*, he says. This is to show that it is not enough to have understood this teaching and to have declared it to be true. We must also, each of us, apply it personally. We must not allow words merely to pass before our eyes or echo in our ears, remembering nothing but *Blessed are those . . . , blessed are those . . .* Our Lord Jesus Christ intends all of this for our instruction. In the first place we must learn to be mild-mannered and patient in every trial. Next, to hunger and thirst, remaining meek even when we are unjustly persecuted though we have done no wrong. Lastly, we must learn to have pity on those who suffer, and be sincerely moved to help them as ability and opportunity allow. We must do all these things, without forgetting the word *now* which St Luke adds. This means that although God allows us to experience in this transient life the truth of his Son's teaching, its joyful fulfilment is kept for us until the last day. Let us, then, learn *now* – that is, amid the perplexities of this earthly life – to have pity on those who suffer, and also to suffer ourselves, so that if we are troubled and afflicted, we remain gentle and kind, however much cruelty and brutality may be used against us.

At the last we will surely find that the one who spoke these words possesses all power; all dominion has been given him, and he will accomplish everything we read of in this passage, when he receives us into that heavenly union for which we now yearn.

I have a short announcement to make. The Town Councillors have agreed that our brother N, who has lately served as minister in Jussy, should be called to this city. He is to be presented on Sunday next. Since all church members have the right to be heard, anyone who has an objection concerning him should declare it to the Councillors between now and Sunday.[18]

Now let us cast ourselves down before the majesty of our good God, acknowledging our sins, and beseeching him to give us grace so to admit our faults that we may come to hate them. May we be made anew, so that we may overcome all our passions and tread down all desires of the flesh. May we make it our goal to follow the rule revealed to us by our good Master, and may we give ourselves to him in the expectation that he will be faithful and will keep the promises he has made to us. And may that expectation sustain us until our life's course is done. Therefore together let us say, Almighty God and heavenly Father . . .

4

THE PRICE OF PEACE

Blessed are those who are pure in heart, for they will see God.
⁹ Blessed are those who make peace, for they will be called children
of God. ¹⁰ Blessed are those who are persecuted on account of right-
eousness, for the kingdom of heaven is theirs (Matt. 5:8–10).

Blessed will you be when men hate you, and cast you out, and
speak slander against you, and reject your name as evil for the Son
of man's sake. ²³ Rejoice on that day, and leap for joy. For behold,
your recompense is great in heaven; for their fathers did the same
things to the prophets (Luke 6:22–23).

*E*veryone readily agrees that the best quality anyone can possess is purity of heart and complete honesty. Without these things, every other virtue, however highly regarded, is but stuff and nonsense in God's sight. We all praise integrity, but the sad truth is we fail to follow its precepts. For we soon observe that without cunning and a little roguery it is impossible to live among men. There is no other way, we believe, to avoid trouble, because wicked men are always ready to snare and entrap us. We therefore tell ourselves that we must do as they do.

That is why all of us, having cast our vote for sincerity and transparency and purity of heart, promptly fall away: we play the hypocrite, and use craft and deceit to attain our ends. So when our Lord Jesus Christ says *Blessed are those who are pure in heart*, he is at first glance expressing a commonly held opinion. If, however, we consider how men normally behave, how they delight in cunning and in bent and crooked ways, we must concede that Christ was right to remind his disciples of the importance of honesty and integrity. He goes on to add: *they will see God*. He speaks in this fashion because there are clever but perverse people who are adept at protecting their own interests and who are prepared, if need be, to hoodwink others. No detail escapes them: they run here and there, delving deep into this and that; whenever we have anything to do with them, we find them so persuasive in the way they argue, so expert in the role they play, that we let down our guard. That is how they give the impression of being pure in heart.

But consider, firstly, this. They live such private lives that no one can get close enough to discover what they are really up to. They are so devious it is impossible for anyone to size them up. Then too, they love – as the proverb goes – to fish in troubled waters, and to dabble in things where it is not easy to tell good from bad. The world counts such people as clever. They are indeed much more knowing than the children of God – but what darkness fills their hearts! Believers, by comparison, are judged to be simple-minded folk, scarcely able to decide what to do for the best. They take no pleasure in guile, and very often let pass the opportunity for personal gain or profit. Why? Because they have no experience of the little tricks which many use to catch their victims, first one, then another. They deliberately close their eyes to such things, for they have no desire to profit from someone else's loss.[1]

That, then, is why our Lord says, by way of reply, that if the world mocks our innocence and if by our innocence we seem to lose more than we gain, we should rejoice in a greater reward – seeing God. Our eyes may never be sharp enough to show us where worldly advantage, comfort, convenience, pleasure, and prestige lie, nor how we might reach for them. When we fix our gaze on other things instead, we will be given that clearer vision which is promised to us here: we will rejoice in the presence of God, in whom are found all our blessedness, joy, and glory.

To debate at length how we may see God is, of course, the mark of idle curiosity. Since God's essence is spiritual, we cannot behold him with our physical eyes. Nor, strictly speaking, do we attribute sight to spirit-beings. We might note first, however, that the angels who have no body are nevertheless able to contemplate God's majesty. This is what we read later on, when our Lord Jesus Christ says that the little children have angels to serve them, and that these gaze upon the face of the Father in heaven.[2] It is true that we cannot at present see God, for to see him we would have to be like him, as St John says in his first Epistle.[3] We are a long way from that! The joy of seeing God which our text speaks of here cannot be ours before the last day, when we will be conformed to God's glory.

How then is it possible for our bodies to bear some likeness to the infinite majesty of God, since it is spiritual in essence? To inquire too deeply into such things would be to go beyond our limits. Let us resolve simply to press on, knowing that, once our course is finished, God will show us how it is in his kingdom.

Many today, in a silly, compulsive wish to know, ask what kind of glory believers will have in paradise, whether they will stand or be seated or move about, whether they may still enjoy the created things of earth, to what point and to what end. In short, they love to indulge in useless speculation, to pass through every room in paradise in the hope of seeing what goes on there. But they have no desire to draw near to paradise themselves! We, on the other hand, are already on our way. So let us continue on, always on, as long as we are in this world, and when we have reached our inheritance, then we will know what heaven is like. Suppose a man wanted to buy a house thirty miles away, and promptly sat down and said, 'Well now, I'd like to know what the house is made of, how commodious it is, and how it is situated.' If, for all that, he refused to visit the house, how laughable it would be! So we must all learn to grow stronger in our knowledge of God, so that that we might worship him purely, place our confidence in him, and call on him in every necessity. And when we have profited by being trained up in these things, we will finally understand what God's promise of blessedness and joy really means and how far it extends. At present, to be sure, the manner of God's working is unknown to us, since Scripture declares that the mind cannot conceive what God has prepared for us.[4]

In the meantime, it is enough to know that the Lord Jesus Christ forbids his disciples to practise craftiness and to seek more light than is permissible. For by such means we appear wiser than we are, deceiving some and cheating others. We may not perhaps succeed as the world counts success, for we behave with integrity. We may let many opportunities for gain pass us by. We will willingly accept loss if by our actions we risk offending God. Since, then, we are people of peaceable spirit, and have neither wit nor skill to fish in troubled waters, we are bound to lose out. We know, however, that while the world may condemn us, we have a recompense which fully satisfies: we will have God to enjoy. For the word 'see' in Scripture means 'enjoy'. When Scripture says *You will not see death*, or *You will not see the kingdom of heaven*, it is the same as saying, 'you will not possess it.'

Our Lord Jesus Christ is actually telling us that God will be our inheritance, provided we have obtained nothing by crooked dealing, have steered clear of evil, have not pursued destructive schemes or sought maximum advantage for ourselves. He tells us too that we will have no cause to regret what we have done. And why? Is there not ample reward in the fact that God declares that he is ours, that he desires to be our inheritance and to make us his?

Where else is true happiness and blessing to be found if not here? Christ thus applies the metaphor of sight, according to normal scriptural usage, because he is speaking here of a heart which is pure. The more our heart is cleansed of evil, the more honest and upright it is, and the less prone we are to sinful dealing. By contrast, those who are steeped in darkness and who are therefore blind, are much more clear-sighted in such things. Clear-sighted? Yes, but they see differently – out of the corner of their eyes, like those who peek through holes so as not to appear in the open. So here our Lord uses this metaphor to teach that, if we fail to 'see' what men naturally covet, God will indeed reveal himself to us; as we lay hold of him, he will give us rest.

Our Lord next adds, *Blessed are the peace-makers*. This word has been commonly misunderstood. It has been interpreted as meaning the 'peaceful', whereas a much stronger sense is implied. A man might indeed be peaceful, without being a peace-maker – that is, without pursuing peace with others. The word is a composite one: 'peace' and 'make'.[5] To avoid ambiguity, we should stick to the text's natural sense, which is that we should cultivate peace wherever we are. That means that we should begin first with ourselves. After all, how could any of us make peace and calm troubles and disputes when they occur, unless we lead by example?[6]

Imagine a man who is given to quarrelling with everyone and who is impatient and reckless in everything he does. Yet, on hearing some commotion, he turns up and tries to calm things down. 'Enough!' he says, 'Let's have peace!' Or supposing he comes upon a riot, he intervenes and cries: 'Now then, stop all this fighting!' What authority would such a man have when, one minute, he loses his temper and storms and rages, and the next he tries to make peace with those around him? Understand that, to be peacemakers, we must first and foremost be peaceable ourselves. What exactly do I mean? Remember what was earlier said about the meek: meekness is part of being peaceable. If we are patient, it will not be our fault if we do not live in harmony and peace with other men. Why else do men inflict such suffering on one another, and war among themselves, and fight like cats and dogs, if not because they are impatient? No one can bear to be wronged, and we are so addicted to self-interest that we demand instant satisfaction; if we do not get it, we immediately take off the gloves. Then come recrimination and hostility, which turn to mortal hatred and the wish to kill and murder, with no one being spared. That is how impatience prevents men from living peaceably together; that is why we consciously chafe and fret, and why each of us is a devil to his neighbour. We must learn, then, to cultivate patience, and so to lay aside self-interest and reputation that we readily forgive the wrongs done to us. That, I believe, is how we can be peaceable.

For the rest, it is not enough for us to avoid giving people cause to injure or trouble us. We must do whatever we can to keep the peace among ourselves. That is what we must do, even if it means suffering loss as a result or surrendering some of our rights. For peace should be so precious to us – God after all commends it – that nothing else should matter to us.

Imagine someone who takes care not to stir up trouble or annoy anybody, and who instead tries hard to please everyone: whether he is given a hard time or not; he will gently put up with many wrongs rather than make a fuss. Even so, we are bound to follow our Lord's precept here, and strive for peace in every place. So it is not enough to refrain from violence, ill-will or injury to others: when someone is in the wrong, we must resist; when innocent people suffer affliction, we should support them as much as we can, bringing them help and relief. When we see two people at odds with each other, we should feel pity for two souls redeemed by the blood of our Lord Jesus Christ, but who are in danger of perdition.[7] We should grieve when victory goes to the devil, who is the prince of discord, and when God, who is the author of peace, is shut out. That thought should make us want to put an end to quarrelling. That also is why, contrariwise, God curses all who stir up dissension and conflict among men. They are like firebrands, who by their gossip incite former friends to hate each other; and when mutual suspicion is aroused, they sneak in and fan the flames. It is as if there were an open wound, and someone were to come and, instead of applying good ointment as a cure, rubbed in poison or venom, making it flare up even worse.

Be assured, then, that we are, as it were, banished from the school of Christ and his church when we stir up hostility and conflict among men. Conversely, in order to be his disciples, we must not only be peaceable ourselves, but must also try as hard as we can to overcome hostility, to put out the fire once it is lit, and to avoid disputes of every kind. Whenever we see people ready to yield to hatred, we should intervene early to set things right. We should not wait for Satan to win the day; we should get in first. That, briefly put, is what we must grasp.

In order to impress his teaching on us, our Lord declares that those who bring about peace *will be called children of God*. Could anything be better than for God to acknowledge and recognize us as his children, and for us to call upon him as Father? Imagine our situation if that were not so. If God were to reject us, what would we have left? Even if we had all we wanted in this world, would not everything be cursed and spoiled for us, if God were against us? For we can have no true taste of prosperity or blessing unless we experience God's favour and fatherly love toward us. That, then, is what we must truly aim at – knowing God as Father and having the privilege of calling ourselves his children. Moreover we cannot attain this blessing, as Jesus Christ reminds us here, unless we are peace-makers. For God is rightly called the God of peace,[8] and we must be like him, or else we do not belong to him, whatever we profess with our lips. The test of whether God is our Father is that we want to live in obedience to him. That means striving to put an end to all disharmony, so far as lies in our power. I do not deny that we will often be forced to fight against the wicked, or that, while strenuously pursuing peace as St Paul urges us,[9] we will have to endure many shocks and storms. Not only that, but we will frequently be blamed as the authors of trouble and turmoil. That is why our Lord goes on to say, *Blessed are we when we suffer persecution, when men slander and reject us,* hating us and expelling us from the fellowship. *Blessed are we*, provided we suffer above all for the gospel's sake.[10]

That, then, is how God acknowledges us to be his, however much the world calls us rebels and trouble-makers, as if we were to blame for the absence of peace! There are two requirements to be balanced here. First, we must be peaceable, patiently bearing the wrongs done to us, with calmness and meekness of spirit so as not to feed our appetite for combat. Second, we must make peace in every place, even while we fight against the devil who is the father of conflict, tumult, and contention. Have any of us done that? Come what may, nothing should be dearer to us than God's truth.

Then, too, let us fight for the cause of righteousness, that is to say for what is just. It is not enough to make an indiscriminate peace. The basis of peace is the recognition that God rules among men: his rule joins us together so that we serve him with one accord. Those who use violence and aggression to get their way must be restrained and the rights of the innocent upheld. Indiscriminate peace is different. Today, for example, when disputes arise, would-be know-it-alls who bravely play the role of peacemaker rush to reach a settlement – any kind of settlement – without first considering who is right and who is wrong. 'Come on', they say, 'let's divide down the middle.' Imagine, on the one hand, a thief ready to slit his brother's throat, and on the other a man who merely wants to keep what is his and protect his rights. Supposing a peace-maker steps between them. 'Now then', he cries, 'stop fighting, and both of you take your share!' Should the thief be allowed to fleece his innocent victim, while others stand idly by, so blind that they cannot tell black from white? This is the lesson we must learn: it is not enough to resolve disputes; justice must always have the last word, must always prevail.

The terms on which peace is to be established are therefore clear. That is why Christ adds the words, *we must be persecuted on account of righteousness.* What he means, in the first place, is that we must defend the rights of all, favouring or excluding no one out of partiality, and being careful to see that everything is done with fairness. Haughty ambition and violence must be put down, and support given to all who want to quietly enjoy what is theirs. That is the first thing to be said.

But if justice is a right owed to men, what is that compared to God's justice, compared, that is, to his truth, which is the measure of all righteousness? If we must endure hatred, abuse, and blame for siding with the innocent and the humble, we need to be even more zealous in our witness to God, resisting those who blaspheme against his truth or who corrupt in any way the teaching of the gospel, on which our welfare and salvation depend. That is why these two things – righteousness or equity, gospel and truth – are joined together. Our Lord speaks first in general terms about righteousness, and then about the Son of man and the gospel. He means us to do justice to all men, but above all to make his truth our first priority, together with the Father's glory and the kingdom which he has received. All these must come before anything else.

As peace-makers, we lay ourselves open to attack from every side. At the very least people will demand that we support them by acting as their defenders and advocates. If we are scrupulously fair and have no bias toward either party, we will inevitably attract criticism from both. As a general rule we find that when those who strive to be God's servants arbitrate a dispute, they end up pleasing no one. It is easy to see why. More often than not the parties are interested not in the pros and cons of the case but in defeating their neighbour and in getting ahead of everyone else. That is how it is. When we openly affirm that we are for the rights of the innocent, attacks against us redouble. Why? Because in the normal course of events it is people of standing and authority who are in the wrong. I mean the powerful and the rich, those on whom society fawns. The result is bitter, drawn-out conflict.

There are of course poor people who are just as bad as the rich: if they had the chance to spit out the venom they secrete, they would prove no less wicked than the rich. The fact remains, however, that the mischief they do is nothing compared to the evil done by those who trust in reputation and wealth, and who are powerful among men.[11] Therefore, if we intend to defend justice and righteousness, we will have to take the fight to those whose sword, so to speak, is already in their hand, to those well able to smite and punish us, though we have done them no wrong.

There is an urgent need for us to put this teaching into practice. Our Lord is not here dealing with things unfamiliar or unusual. He is telling us how we should be spending every moment of our lives. Naturally, when we live blamelessly and do nothing to upset our neighbour, no one should have cause to hate us; we should be left in peace, out of harm's way. Indeed, St Peter says, 'If you wrong no one, who can be your enemy?'[12] That is as it should be. Nevertheless God's children, after showing much patience and after striving to resolve disputes, must be prepared to suffer many attacks and slanders and to be the unwitting cause of many troubles.

The reason is, as I have said, that if we stand up for what is right, we are bound to arouse the fury of many people. Many more will follow in their wake. The more we make peace, the readier the world will be to revile us. Our name will be bandied around every table and every street in town. Scurrilous things will be said about us. But there is more. St Paul tells us that anyone desiring to live a holy life in Jesus Christ must expect persecution.[13] God, it is true, will certainly give us respite from time to time, but we cannot avoid making many enemies. Satan has many allies in this world: possessed by his spirit, they cannot endure the light of the gospel or allow God to rule over them as one might rule over children. We must therefore defend the cause of the gospel and bear witness to the truth of our Lord Jesus Christ, even if it means unremitting struggle with a large number of people, including those who pretend to be believers and who claim to be of the same religion. We are engaged, I repeat, in a mortal struggle with them, and even more with those who openly defy God and who would love to see the gospel vanish from the world.

This is a lesson we need to thoroughly absorb if we are not to puzzle over the wrongs we often suffer. For there are many people who believe they have made great progress in the gospel but who, if attacked, never fail to advance this excuse: 'I never gave him cause for offence. Why does he fly at me this way, seeing I've done nothing to him? Wasn't I right to rebuff him?' They imagine they are blameless, even though their conduct has been highly reckless.

Now Scripture says something very different. It says that we may indeed be meek of heart, zealous for justice and righteousness, but that men will nevertheless oppose us and hostility will abound, especially when we are devoted to God's glory and to the truth of the gospel. There will be open warfare, and we will be blamed for everything which goes wrong. So today the papists quote the text, *Blessed are the peace-makers*, when they want to impugn and blame us for causing all the trouble, strife, and quarrels in the world. They believe they would be free to exercise their tyranny, and that men would fall in with their idolatrous inventions, if only we stopped raising a hue and cry against such abominations. That is why they say we are disturbers of the peace and enemies of the church.

Be that as it may, remember what I said earlier: the war we fight has to do with God's honour, and also with rights and mutual justice among men. It has to do especially with our testimony to the Lord Jesus Christ and with the doctrine of our salvation. That is how we are to approach the fight – we are for righteousness, that is, for a cause which is right and necessary. To be at peace with everybody we would have to turn our backs on God. Since that is so, on what basis could we possibly agree with the papists? What understanding could we come to? They would be delighted to have us on their side, but on what terms? We would have to become apostates like them, shut out of the kingdom of God; we would have to join them in their foul, putrid cesspool; in a word, we would have to become the devil's children, as they are.[14]

That, I say, is how they would like to seduce and catch us if they could. God forbid that we should have peace at such a price! War would be better, provided it was for the testimony which pleases God, provided we fought under his banner, provided he was worshipped and honoured, provided we were content to suffer men's enmity. Provided, too, any rift from our side was because we had no time for the sins and profanity of the wicked.

It is important, at this point, to look at the word 'righteousness'. To be sure, the wicked might boast that because they too suffer, they should be regarded as disciples of Christ. In former times, we know, there were heretics who proudly boasted that their faith was genuine, on the grounds that everyone was persecuting them. Today, also, those crackpots, the Anabaptists, who cause so much trouble in the world, who denounce governments, magistrates, the unity of the church, and who scatter everywhere the terrible seeds of error, never tire of repeating this phrase, *Blessed are those who suffer persecution.*[15] Yes, but do they suffer on account of righteousness? The answer is no: the opposite is true. We should have the word 'righteousness' firmly written on our hearts, and ensure that, whenever we are persecuted, our conscience testifies before God that our cause is just. For that is the mark chosen by Christ to distinguish his disciples from those who are brigands, thieves, murderers, blasphemers, and adulterers. The wicked indeed suffer persecution, and we ought to punish them as severely as we can, as David declares in the Psalm, when he says that he hates them for their iniquities, not for themselves.[16]

It is necessary, then, to punish the wicked, but that does not give them the right to boast that God will therefore uphold them. They are not suffering on account of righteousness, as Christ's witnesses and martyrs do; nor are they suffering like those who in this world always defend what is right, who insist on supporting the innocent and who lift them up when they are oppressed. These too suffer on account of righteousness, and bear the mark by which God recognizes them as his.

Time, unfortunately, does not allow a more thorough treatment of this theme. It is enough here if we note how important it is to be peace-makers, provided we do not prejudice God's honour or glory or bring reproach to his name. We should above all cherish the peace made known to us in the gospel, in that Christ has made peace between us and his Father, who now commands that reconciliation be preached between God and man. St Paul reminds us of this when he urges us to have done with all dissensions, divisions, and false opinions. How is this possible, he asks? By being reconciled to God, and so maintaining brotherhood among us.[17] This is accomplished by the preaching of the gospel.

Therefore we who claim to have received the message which reconciles us to God, should so live as to encourage peace and harmony among men. And if this duty is laid on everyone, it is laid much more on those who are in positions of authority. But again, this requires a longer exposition than is possible here.

It so happens that we have among us a brother who has served our church as minister in another place. He has been accepted by the Town Councillors and appointed from now on to serve in this city. Every time a minister is inducted, we must remember to what end those called to the ministry labour among us, and how we may benefit from their labours. This is the sum and substance of it: while we were still enemies of God, he called to us and early found us, not waiting for us to seek him out; seeing us lost, in a state of perdition, he sought us out and called us to himself. This he did by forgiving all our sins, so that we in turn might learn to forgive our neighbour's sins. He desires to treat us with pity, so that we might treat others with pity.

Let us then carefully consider to what end and for what purpose the gospel is preached, and the blessings God offers us in its teaching. The gospel is set before us in his name: let all of us, great and small, be stirred up to obey and to do our duty. Moreover, since we cannot be counted as God's children unless we are peace-makers, let us continually profit from the teaching we receive. The devil will always find ways to goad us into quarrelling, evil-doing, warring and upsetting the peace. We need to strive with might and main, because when we try to preserve peace and harmony, we are up against our own nature. We can succeed only when we are committed to God's teaching, and only when we give it the earnest attention it deserves.

Since, as well as peace-makers, we need to be both upright and fervent in heart, we must value God's truth above all else. The word perfectly proclaimed by Jesus Christ should be so familiar to us that we do not fear to offend the whole world. Now in this respect we are so cold that what Isaiah said of his generation could be said of us: 'Look up and down the streets, there is no one who defends what is right; no one upholds truth.'[18] Why, you ask, is that? Because, first, we do not understand how much God loves integrity and justice. And second, because we fail to see how precious his truth is to him. Contempt for God's Word and for what it can do for us makes us forsake justice and integrity, however much we might claim to respect them. Of course we lament, and say: 'Just look at the times we are living in! The whole world is upside down!' Yet all of us are guilty, one way or another, since we are all tepid and lacklustre. For that reason the word 'righteousness' should always be ringing in our ears, since righteousness is what we stand for. And righteousness, above all, means defending the honour of God's name, and imprinting forever on our hearts the witness we owe to Jesus our Lord.

We should think of these things, then, so as to show that we have come further in the faith than before. In particular, we must understand that Jesus Christ wills to rule his church by the preaching of his Word, to which we must give all due reverence. It is not, however, feigned obedience which is asked of us. Our whole life should testify that we have set our hearts on this treasure beyond belief, and have put behind us all earthly affections which all too easily entrap us.

Now let us cast ourselves down before the majesty of our good God, acknowledging our sins, and beseeching him so to move us by the remembrance of them that we may be led to true repentance. And may he more and more reveal to us the great and terrible transgressions we commit, so that we may seek his forgiveness with ever more fervency. May we also yearn to be born again by his Holy Spirit, until we are wholly conformed to his will. Therefore together let us say, Almighty God and heavenly Father . . .

5

THE REJECTED RECOMPENSED[1]

Blessed will you be when you are insulted and persecuted, when evil things are said and lies told against you, for my sake. *[12] Rejoice and be glad, for your reward is great in heaven. For in the same way they persecuted the prophets who were before you* (Matt. 5:11–12)

You will be blessed when men hate you and reject you and slander you and cast you out as evil, on account of the Son of man. *[23] Be glad on that day and leap for joy, for behold your recompense is great in heaven. For their fathers did the same to the prophets.* *[24] But woe to you who are rich, for you have already obtained your consolation.* *[25] Woe to you who are filled, for you will go hungry. Woe to you who now laugh, for you will lament and weep.* *[26] Woe to you when all men speak well of you, for their fathers did the same with the false prophets* (Luke 6:22–26).

*W*e saw last Sunday that it is not easy for believers to live in peace when they desire to do their duty both to God and their neighbour. For men are so full of mischief that we must often struggle to protect the innocent and the weak when they are afflicted, and to take up just and worthy causes. For that is what God demands of us. It is not enough for us to abstain from wrong

---

[1] This sermon is in part on the same text as the preceding sermon, and in part on the text which follows.

and harmful actions: we must also do good to the best of our ability. The truth is, as I have said, that around us there are many evil-doers. Not for nothing is the devil called the prince of this world. So it is not only hard for us to serve God and to live quietly and peaceably, we must also reckon with the fact that, in defending the good, we will experience many conflicts and alarms. The wicked will be our enemy.

This is especially so when sound doctrine is in view. For men have a settled hatred of God's truth – at least until they are transformed by it! – because those who commit evil cannot abide the light, but rather hate it, as our Lord himself says.[1] Now it is the case that all men are evil, and that evil, if not openly manifest, lies deep within, like a filthy stain. Men are happy to live as hypocrites. God, however, by means of his Word, brings everything to light; he plumbs our hidden thoughts and our most secret desires. That is why men will not receive God's truth, but will reject and resist it as long as they can.

In brief, we are exhorted to remember continually what our Lord Jesus teaches in this passage. When we are unjustly afflicted, provided our conscience testifies before God that we are blameless, we must not lose heart, thinking that we are worse off than unbelievers. Why? Because the happiness we are to seek is from above. While we are on earth, we must prepare to do battle. But there is also the promise of rest which will be ours, of victory and the glory which goes with it. That promise calls us to look away from the world and to lift up our minds to the realm above.

Moreover we are not only encouraged to put up with personal injury and trouble, but also with criticism, slander, and false report. This is perhaps the hardest thing of all to bear, since a brave person will endure beatings and even death more easily than humiliation and disgrace. Among those pagans who had a reputation for courage were noble souls who feared death less than shame and dishonour among men.[2] We, therefore, must arm ourselves with more than human steadfastness if we are to calmly swallow all the insults, censures, and blame which the wicked will undeservedly heap upon us. That, nevertheless, is what awaits us, as St Paul declares. Since, he says, our hope is in the living God, we are bound to suffer distress and humiliation; we will be objects of suspicion; men will spit in our face.[3] That is God's way of testing us. We must therefore be ready to face these things and to take our Lord's teaching here as our shield for the fight.

For the rest, he warns us that reproaches will come not only from those who openly decry the gospel and who have no time for pure and true religion, but also from those who pass themselves off as members of the church and who have every appearance of sincerity: they will be the first to pull us down and to shame us in men's eyes.

That is why Jesus makes a point of saying that his disciples *will be rejected, and driven out, and their name will be accursed*. He says the same thing in St John, declaring that believers and ministers of the gospel will be persecuted by men who believe they are offering God a most pleasing sacrifice.[4] That was how it was in former times under the law, as we read in the eighth chapter of Isaiah.[5] There it is said that God's followers were dismissed as trouble-makers both by the world and by those who posed as champions of the Catholic faith (for so it is called); not only so, but God's followers became a byword for all that is repulsive among men. That is how Isaiah describes them: 'Behold the children whom the Lord has given me', he says. 'They are as objects of dread, designed to inspire men with fear, abhorrent even to nature.' Here we clearly see how Isaiah and those who joined with him in the pure worship of God were rejected. And by whom? Ah! not by the Egyptians or by those who freely confessed to being idolaters, but by the two houses of Israel, by the two kingdoms which had been consecrated to God. For although the ten tribes which split off from David's house, rebelled and in appearance turned away from God, a remnant nevertheless was left in whom God had chosen to be honoured. So it was that something of God's unction remained in that kingdom, as in Judah.[6] Isaiah is thus saying that both of these nations, whose members at that time were held to be the holy church and lineage of Abraham, hated the true prophets and the genuine followers of God.

Therefore, when Jesus Christ appeared and God's truth was more perfectly proclaimed, the devil's wrath and the anger of the wicked grew even hotter and fell with frenzy upon God's children, who suffered persecution and physical distress but also vile abuse, for the charge was made that they threatened the order and good government of God's church.

Now excommunication was a holy institution, designed from the beginning by God to purge his church of all uncleanness. Its purpose was to cut off those who behaved immorally or who caused offence. That was only right, for even the pagans held excommunication in high regard, ashamed to think that the wicked and unclean might take part in the act of sacrifice. That was a sacrilege they could not endure. If poor blind pagans practised such discipline, the same procedure had certainly to be followed in the church of God. Here, then, Jesus Christ maintains that his disciples must inevitably face this kind of test: they will be thrown out of the synagogue, like men condemned, odious and defiled.[7]

The lesson we have to take from this verse is clear. It is the lesson which St Paul teaches us in the passage quoted earlier, namely that we must bear personal suffering and injury with patience, even at the cost of life itself. In such things steadfastness is required. And when we are reviled, furiously assaulted, falsely accused of crimes, we must put our heads down and quietly wait for God to make our innocence shine like the dawn, as Scripture says in another place.[8] We should follow the example of Jeremiah who, calling on God to be his protector and knowing that God approved his cause, was unworried by anything that men could bring against him.[9] So when in the course of this life men cast us out, it is enough for us to know that God still counts us as his servants. Let us therefore walk before him in such a way that the world's reproaches neither lead us into sin nor divert us from the proper path.

This teaching is most necessary for us today, because it is so rarely obeyed and because we could not otherwise understand what it is to serve God. For there are many – not, perhaps, very many – who live good lives and who cannot be accused of greed, theft, immorality or excess of any kind. Everyone commends the way they live. But we need to ask ourselves, What is it that keeps them on so tight a rein? Is it not because they crave reputation and honour? That, I maintain, is the way it is with the fine, respectable people of this world. They are happy to enjoy the appearance of virtue. All that, alas, is mere smoke, since it is men they seek to impress. They have already received their reward, as we will later see.[10]

Contrariwise, when we have striven to live a blameless life and given no one cause to criticize or slander us, and yet suffer humiliation, injury and attack, when we are as men flayed alive, when one of us is denounced as a hypocrite and another as a knave, when, in short, we are the butt of every kind of slander – if, undeterred, we continue on our way, we will truly prove to be God's servants.

Why? Because boasting after the fashion of the world means nothing to us. Here we have a useful test which shows how sincere we are and how keen we are for God's service. It is when we can look up and honestly affirm that our heart is not divided and that we have no interest in the world's vain things; that we have not stopped following the path God has shown us, for that was always what he purposed.

SERMONS ON THE BEATITUDES

We cannot, then, be too careful in observing that however much the wicked may revile us, we must take the path traced out for us by God. We must persevere, for God will surely prove to be our protector, the one who causes our innocence to shine, as the Psalm already quoted promises.

The passage we are examining speaks of excommunication. What our Lord means here is plain for us to see. To the Pope, his cronies and the clerical rabble around them, we are no better than dogs, to be struck down by sentence of excommunication. The truth is that they have been unmasked; in many places they have lost practically all their authority. There is not one papist today who respects these horned beasts or that foul plague of priests (as they are called). Not one, I repeat, in all piety respects them. Everyone knows that they follow man-made fictions. That is why they should be left just as they are, abandoned to their own devices. That will not stop them claiming the titles of prelate and bishop, or flinging their excommunications in our faces.

Imagine, however, what would happen if we did not have our Lord's teaching to fortify us. Events would quite bewilder us. 'How is it', we would be saying, 'that in defending God's truth and in bearing witness to Jesus Christ, the Saviour of the world, we should be driven out, an abomination to men, unworthy even to eke out a living on earth?' As it is, we have the example of the prophets, we see what the apostles and their followers went through. We are not more privileged than they. So let us walk wherever God calls us; his absolution is sufficient for us, even though the whole world should condemn us.

We openly spurn the exclusions pronounced by the Pope and his crew, for we know that the more this riff-raff rejects us, the more God approves of us. And the further we move from their vile practices, the closer we draw to our Lord Jesus Christ and the more we partake of his innocence.

Consider, in this connection, what happened to the man whose sight Jesus restored.[11] He declared that the one who had healed him could not possibly be evil, since God had heard his prayer; therefore God must have sent him, for he was also reputed to be a holy prophet. Now when the poor man had spoken his mind, he was excommunicated, cast out, like a fugitive who deserved no place on earth. He was driven away by that rascally lot who nevertheless revelled in the title of priests of the law and prelates of the church. Yet Jesus returned to meet and talk with him. For our part, we must never doubt that the Son of God will welcome us whenever we are rejected by men and by the devil's henchmen. Their only aim is to plunge the world into such confusion that no one will be able to tell God from an idol, or true religion from false.

That, briefly, is what we must we must grasp here. We must not count our lives as precious when, by bearing witness to the truth, we experience affliction, for truth is the key to our salvation, happiness, and hope of glory. So when we suffer loss of reputation, we should not cling to our good name by attempting to evade the reproaches aimed at us. We will endure, provided we maintain our walk with God and have the proofs of his approval; provided, too, our conscience answers for us, as St Peter says.[12] St Paul writes elsewhere in the same vein that we should expect to be denounced and reviled, but should not grow tired of doing good.[13]

Let men treat us then as evil-doers: we will go on regardless, maintaining our integrity. God will be witness and judge of our sincerity. If in the meantime men accuse us of wrong-doing and trample over us, let us press on, giving offence to none and doing good to all, but always ready to suffer abuse, to be condemned, and rejected. Condemned and rejected? Yes, we are as guilty men, under attack from all sides. That is what our passage teaches. Jesus Christ sets before us, as he set before his disciples, the example of the prophets. We therefore have a double model – both prophets and disciples. If persecution were unprecedented, if God's servants had never before been abused or cast out, even the hardiest might have trembled and contemplated ruin. That is why it was important for believers to know that such things were neither new nor cause for wonder.

The prophets were outstanding men, possessing such exceptional powers that they were like angels sent by God to earth. Our Lord refers to them as if to say to his disciples, 'You are in no way superior to them. They represented God's very person; they bore the mark of his majesty, so that everyone stood in awe of them. Yet how were they treated? They suffered not only much physical abuse but slanders and insults; they were condemned as rebels and enemies of the church. We know how Jeremiah was accused of trying to stir up trouble and strife among the people, of being a traitor in league with his country's enemies. He was promptly thrown into prison and went through every possible indignity.[14] Isaiah, too, was put to death in the cruellest of ways. Some were scourged and others torn limb from limb. All this they suffered, because God had given them power to endure. Why, then, should you expect a better fate?' What happened to the prophets was thus a salutary lesson for our Lord's disciples. When tried by battle and under fierce attack they were not to bend and break but always to push forward. Much the same lesson is found in St Peter.[15] He exhorts us to continue on, though conflicting opinions and arguments may bar our way, and heretics try to ruin us by muddling and upsetting everything. Such things trouble and confuse many who are weak. Well, says St Peter, have you not heard that in the church of old there were always false prophets who laid claim to that venerable and holy office and who professed to speak in God's name? Yet did believers desert the faith on that account? No, never. They knew that the truth would triumph, and that even if it were attacked from every side they must not flinch from following it.

So when we see how God's followers remained faithful despite the disorders in the church, we know what to do when false teachers arise. We must hold our ground and not be like those who weakly lament: 'Whom can we trust?' Let us look instead to God and, mindful of what he has done in the past, let us reflect on how from the beginning he has guided his church. For our part, we should walk with integrity and humility. If we do that, we can be sure that God will keep us from going astray. Such, then, is our task. And however much the world may rage against the gospel, we should stand fast and learn what it means to follow both the prophets and our Lord's disciples and apostles. We, today, have a firmer confidence than the disciples had: their only model was the prophets. But we have the apostles, the disciples, and the example of all who have come after them. We have a greater resource to strengthen and comfort us when we are unjustly persecuted – persecuted even by men who falsely invoke God's name and pass themselves off as pillars of the church!

Our Lord's words might, however, have left us feeling despondent had he not gone on to say more in St Luke. Believers are warned to prepare for persecution, rejection, slander, ignominy, and disgrace; they know that they may be treated as criminals. Even so, they would be less than human not to draw a comparison with others. 'Just look at those who mock God,' they might say, 'respectable people, popular, everyone's favourite! Here we are, the scum of the earth, rejected and despised, hated by all! The wicked, who make no secret of their contempt for God, who live immoral lives and are enemies of good order, are left undisturbed, fawned upon, feted wherever they go. While they eat the finest food and appear the happiest of men, all we do is groan and weep, hunger and thirst, while they make gluttons of themselves!'

Such thoughts might well give Jesus' followers cause for regret. The idea is well expressed in the Psalm we have sung.[16] There,

David declares that his foot slipped as if on ice: he was close to stumbling when he saw how the wicked prospered. Ordinary ills, he says, do not touch them. No one dares to notice when they make others suffer, everyone trembles when they are near. Such things might have quite overwhelmed him had not God held him up. Yet victory did not come quickly, for by his own admission he was like a brute beast, like an ass or a young ox which has lost its way and cannot be controlled.

Our Lord Jesus Christ foresaw the difficulties our anxious minds conceive. He therefore adds, *Woe, woe to all who today laugh. Woe to all who have eaten their fill. Woe to all who are loved by the world.* His purpose is to teach us to await finality and not to judge on first appearances. The blessedness we attribute to the wicked is a dream, as is this present life. Though God should grant the wicked every possible pleasure and comfort, they cannot avoid, sometime or other, bitter disappointments, since God gives them due warning that good times will not last. He thus removes any possibility of excuse, so that they may acknowledge their misdeeds and be ready to account for them. Their condemnation will be all the greater if they do not heed God's warnings.

Therefore, whatever the pleasures, pomp, sensual delights, honours, wealth, and possessions enjoyed by the worldly and the profane, these are an illusion which will shortly vanish. That is not, of course, how it first seems to us, which is why we are unhappy and depressed when we see the wicked flourish. We envy them, and judge according to what our eyes now see. Our minds are earth-bound.

In order to correct the twisted logic of which we are all too fond, Christ asserts that to equate laughter, a fully satisfied appetite, and wealth with blessedness, is to ignore the end result, to rush heedlessly to judgment, and to decide matters on the flimsiest of evidence.

He keeps us, then, on a short rein, which was his object when he earlier declared: 'You should not feel wretched when you weep, or are hungry or thirsty, or are harassed and persecuted. You should not think of yourself as a worthless creature whom God has abandoned. Why? Because you must pass beyond this world and seek your reward in heaven. Reflect on what it really means to be a child of God, once he becomes your Father and once you claim him as such. That is blessing greater than anyone could desire. As for the wicked, you see them revelling in their good fortune, absorbed in a life of blissful pleasure. Today that is how you see them. But be patient! Their joy will give way to the gnashing of teeth, and their wealth will turn to poverty – for these things are under God's curse. If their worldly dignity serves only to condemn them in the sight of God and his angels, why should you envy them?'

That, in sum, is how our Lord Jesus Christ would have us rise above earthly things and the limits of this transitory life. He reveals that if we cannot have our reward on earth, we should not lose heart, for our reward is in heaven. By saying that our reward is in heaven, he does not mean that it is a recompense which we have earned. The papists, it is true, have a field day with these words, whenever the term 'reward' comes up. Straight away we hear the cry, 'So our works can merit eternal life after all! When we sin, we can make satisfaction and clear ourselves of guilt. And although God's grace is there to help, we can add to our worth by our own efforts.' They concede when pressed that human worth is never equal to the infinite blessing of eternal life. Nevertheless, they believe there is a certain compatibility and agreement between the two. God, they feel, would be unjust if he failed to reward those who have served him well.[17]

The word 'reward' thus gives the papists an apparent excuse to obscure Christ's grace, and even to extinguish it, if that were possible. We, for our part, are sure that our Lord did not come to pander to our pride and arrogance, or to make us authors of our salvation on the false assumption that if we sin, we can readily make amends. There are plenty of other passages where he clearly reveals that salvation is found only in him, and that it is only out of his Father's unmerited goodness that our works have any importance at all. If God counts any of them good – for in themselves they are corrupt, unworthy of acceptance – it is because of his sheer grace, his generosity and his fatherly love toward us.

We see, then, that our Lord's intention here was not to question the basis of our salvation, or to ask what value anything we do for God might have. His object was to show that, if in seeking to do the Father's will we find that men hate us, cast us out and persecute us, our efforts to do good are not wasted. The trials we face should not stop us following our appointed path. Why? Because to serve God on earth involves much conflict. Where, then, does victory lie? In heaven – it is to heaven we must look. Let us set our sights not on winning merit, but on steadfastly walking in God's service. We have a reward, one won for us by our Lord Jesus Christ and which is ours through the merit of his death and passion. There we have merit which cannot fail!

With boldness, then, let us oppose those popish upstarts who talk boastfully about merit but who, in reality, hold God up to contempt. They parade their merits with an assurance that seems to promise miracles. To hear them speak, you would think they burned with fervent zeal. Yet not one would lift a finger if it meant suffering a little for Christ's sake. Don't expect them to live a life of patient self-denial. Those best known for preaching about merit, those dumb, misguided bigots who make the loudest din, are immoral rascals, dissolute and worldly, or else drunken and depraved. They are guilty of every evil and excess. So much for the Pope's men, who bravely preach about merit but whose lives are an affront to God!

What about us? Our good deeds might exceed God's standard a hundred times over. We would be wrong, however, to think that we had gone beyond the call of duty. We must frankly admit that we owe everything we are to God. And since we are accountable to him in everything, what debt can he possibly owe us? What obligation can he have toward us? Understand also that even when we mean to do good, we limp and shuffle, we are in no hurry. Our intentions are always flawed, always we fall short. Everyone who is not a hypocrite admits as much. So we conclude that all our works would merit God's curse, except that in his great goodness he chooses to approve them, since we are disciples of Jesus Christ and have reposed our trust in him. That, then, is how we can really profit from Jesus' teaching. God draws us towards heaven so as to make it easier for us to walk among thorns, leap ditches, and even scale rocks and mountains when we have to. Nothing should get in our way, nothing should stop us pressing towards our goal.

Someone might ask whether it is right for God's children to be rich, to employ the good things which God so generously gives and to derive pleasure from them. After all, our text says *Woe to you who laugh. Woe to you rich. Woe to you when men speak well of you.* 'What's this?' you say. 'Is it wrong to lead a good and virtuous life and to be well spoken of? Doesn't St Paul urge us to do good in the sight of all? Don't we read somewhere else that every mouth should be stopped and that men should glorify God when they see us walking in his fear?'[18] We might, then, think it harsh and puzzling that the rich, the comfortably off, and the happy should be condemned.

Now that is not what our Lord is saying here. What he is condemning is the attitude of those who, intent on living well in this world, are so stupid and senseless as to forget there is a heavenly kingdom. This will be clearer if we think of how believers behave when times are good. If God sends them peace and prosperity, they will give him the praise; they will use his gifts soberly, endeavouring always to live an upright life. They will not want to squander such gifts, but they will recognize them as blessings from God. Or again, if someone possesses a rare gift of God's Spirit, he will not pretend he doesn't have it, for that would be mere hypocrisy. So whether believers are rich, or in robust health, or wonderfully endowed with the Spirit's gifts, they acknowledge that God's favour is its only source. Their joy is real, and so is their thanksgiving. That is how they will use the good things of this present life.[19]

Nevertheless, while life for believers may be easy today, they will be ready tomorrow to endure whatever afflictions God may send them. He may, perhaps, take from them the goods he has given. They are prepared to surrender them, since they know they received them on one condition – that they should hand them back whenever God should choose. The believer reasons this way: 'Rich today, poor tomorrow. If God should change my circumstances so that ease gives way to suffering and laughter to tears, it is enough to know that I am still his child. He has promised to acknowledge me always as his, and in that I rest content.'

That, I repeat, is how believers will behave. They will live soberly, tightening their belts if that is necessary; they will be self-controlled, telling themselves that though they may rise to eminent rank and enjoy untold pleasure, they must set their sights on higher things. The good things given by God are but a path to lead us to him, a ladder to ascend on high, not a tomb in which to bury ourselves. We should not cling to happiness or greet its passing with a hollow laugh, for it is fleeting. Nor should we exult when men applaud us, as if we had already attained our reward for a virtuous life on earth. No, we are determined to press on through good report and bad. Such is the measured and moderate path pursued by the believer. We do not get drowsy, still less intoxicated, when times are good. And we are always willing to abandon everything if God requires. This is not how it is with unbelievers. Prosperity goes immediately to their heads, fills them to bursting; they are so befuddled that not once do they spare a thought for God or the spiritual life. In time they grow hard, and when misfortune comes they grind their teeth and blaspheme against God.

This is how we are to interpret the woes spoken against the rich, the satisfied, those who laugh and are glad. Remember Job, who amidst his suffering proclaimed: 'If we have received good things from God's hand, why should we not also receive the bad?'[20] There is no doubt that this was something which Job had thought hard about – a treasure, so to speak, to be disclosed at the right time and place. We see then that although God may spare us and give us reason to rejoice, we should expect to receive both good and bad from his hand. Not reluctantly or because we are compelled, but meekly and cheerfully, obedient to his will. For he must rule us, not according to our own likes but according to what he knows is best and most expedient for us. We are confident that all things will work for our salvation: that is our motive for rejoicing.

That is the sense of Jesus' teaching in this passage. To be rich, to be glad, to be satisfied is to be drunk on prosperity and to live the life of senseless beasts. If we are comfortably off, it is not so that we may cover ourselves with gold and silver, or boast of owning fields and meadows, like those whose goal in life is to have everything they want. Those kinds of people are as good as dead: they bury themselves in their perishable possessions and are incapable of seeing heaven above. As for us, we must take heed to ourselves lest the Son of God condemn us with his own lips: only by looking to him for continual blessing can we escape the misfortune promised here. We are taught, then, to pass through this world as strangers, convinced, as St Paul says, that those who have should be as those who have not.[21] No one would deny that those who have plenty to live on meet many more temptations and run more risk of falling. They need, therefore, to turn constantly to God, and to learn that his gifts are meant to draw them closer to him, to quicken their love and to encourage their obedience. The good things they receive must never bewitch them to the point that they become captives to the world.

In the midst of plenty we must guard against greedy excess, lest we choke ourselves and bring this curse upon us: *Woe to you who are filled.* If we are to be filled, it is in a different way – by contemplating God's face, as we read in Psalm 16.[22] We should regard material possessions simply as props to help us, until we see the Father face to face. He is our bliss and happiness. By all means let us laugh, but in the manner of those who are ready to weep should that be God's will. Our joy should be joined with sadness, and with compassion for those who suffer. No one should live apart from others, and all should rejoice whenever God's name is honoured. Yes, rejoice, even when we have reason to feel sad and gloomy. Conversely, it may be that we are fine, in the best of spirits. But supposing there is some dire trouble in the church, or God's name is blasphemed, held up to shame or ridicule – that should give us cause for grief, grief deeper even than the joy we felt. At such a time we ought to moderate the happiness which earthly blessings bring. We ought, as the proverb says, to mix water with our wine. So much for the meaning of that verse.

Now consider our Lord's closing words, *Rejoice when men speak ill of you.* He does not mean all men everywhere, but the general run of men. We see this in St Paul, who writes that if he were to serve and please men, he would have to renounce God.[23] For in their fleshly nature men want only to be flattered and humoured. To heap worldly praise on people is to shut one's eyes to their failings, to act as their defenders and advocates, to back them up and to call evil good. That is what happens when we seek men's approval: we corrupt God's truth and wickedly pervert it, and in the process cease to serve our Master.

There is, however, another way by which we may please men. Instead of pandering to their evil nature, we may try to please them God's way, when they themselves despair of the evil they do. That is what St Paul has in mind. Our efforts to please men can only work when they themselves condemn their evil ambitions and their wicked desires. If that is how they feel, God's truth will be acceptable to them, and so will we who are bearers of his truth. If, however, men are left to their fallen nature, they try to cover everything up and insist we turn a blind eye to their sins. So when our Lord uses the word 'men', he means all who are joined in a kind of conspiracy: 'Spare us, and you'll be our friend for life.' That is how worldly men who hate the truth, that is how the hypocrites who have no living root of godly fear, collude with the false prophets. 'We will honour you,' they say, 'we will give you anything you like, as long as you don't upset us by what you say. We won't trouble you if you don't trouble us.'

Was there ever a more detestable conspiracy? Prophets and teachers of the church whose task is to instruct – mere fiddlers, playing sweet songs which tickle the ears of their audience but which achieve nothing! Meantime the flatterers are lavish in their praise: 'Ah! An outstanding teacher! An excellent man! What more could we ask for?' So while some crave compliments and others tell them what they want to hear, our Lord Jesus Christ gives the lie to all such notions: *Woe to you when men speak well of you.* 'In the end', he says, 'you will see that the false prophets deceived you with their flattering words. Cursed are you if the world speaks well of you.'

Note, finally, that this last verse has a particular word of warning for those charged with proclaiming God's Word. If, in trying to do good and to fulfil their duty, they should arouse men's hatred, or come in for criticism or slander, they must not give up but must steadily press on. Now that is something which applies to all of us; it is teaching useful to every member of the church. What I mean is that we should cease praising and applauding men who achieve popularity merely through the use of flattery. We should not look up to them and admire them – unless we want God to condemn us for siding with evil! Instead, let us learn to praise those who have no time for the fame and esteem which flattery confers, and who reject anything which gets in the way of duty.

If we apply ourselves to that, we will fulfil what is said in the Psalms: we will bless those who come in the name of the Lord,[24] until at length he gathers us into his eternal kingdom, where we will taste all the blessings which he has promised us and for which we now wait.

Now let us cast ourselves down before the majesty of our good God, acknowledging our sins, and beseeching him to give us a conscience which so abhors them that we may more and more cast them away, and be clothed with his righteousness, until we attain its true perfection. Therefore together let us say, Almighty God and heavenly Father . . .

PRAYER AFTER THE SERMON[1]

*A*lmighty God and heavenly Father, you have promised to hear and answer our requests which we make to you in the name of your beloved Son, Jesus Christ our Lord. We are further taught by him and his apostles to gather together in his name, with the promise that he will be among us and will intercede for us before you, that we may receive and obtain all things on which we are agreed on earth.

You bid us pray, first, for those whom you have set up over us, our leaders and governors. Next, for the needs of all your people, and of all men everywhere. Therefore, trusting in your holy truth and in your promise, and being assembled here before you in Jesus' name, we lovingly beseech you, our God and Father, in your infinite mercy, freely to pardon our transgressions, and so to lift our thoughts and desires to you that we may heartily call upon you according to your good will and pleasure. We therefore pray, heavenly Father, for all princes and lords, your servants to whom you have committed the rule of justice.

Most particularly do we pray for the rulers of this city, that you will endue them with your Spirit, who alone is gracious and sovereign, and daily increase his gifts in them, that they, acknowledging your Son Jesus Christ to be King of kings and Lord of lords, with full power in heaven and on earth, may

---

[1] The Sunday sermon was followed by a long prayer of intercession, said by the minister and concluding with an extended paraphrase of the Lord's Prayer. Our translation follows the Genevan liturgy of 1542, omitting the paraphrase. Text in *CO* 6. 175–8; *OS* 2. 20–3.

seek to serve him and exalt his reign in all their dominions, and may according to your will, guide and govern their subjects, who are the work of your hands and the sheep of your pasture. And may we, your people, here and everywhere, being kept in peace and tranquillity, serve you in holiness and righteousness. And, free from the fear of our enemies, may we give you praise all our days.

We pray also, true Father and Saviour, for all whom you have ordained as pastors to your people, who have the care of souls and the administration of your holy gospel. May you lead and direct them by your Holy Spirit, that they may be found faithful and true ministers of your glory, always striving to gather and bring home the erring and wayward sheep to the Lord Jesus Christ, our chief Shepherd and principal Bishop, that they might daily prosper and grow in him in all righteousness and holiness. Grant, moreover, that all churches may be delivered from the mouths of ravening wolves and hirelings, who follow their own purposes and ambitions, and have no care for the honour of your holy name and the welfare of your flock.

Next we pray, most gracious God and merciful Father, for all men generally. Since you desire all men to acknowledge you as Saviour of the world, through the redemption won by our Lord Jesus Christ, may those who do not know him, being in darkness and captive to ignorance and error – may they by the light of your Holy Spirit and the preaching of your gospel, be led into the way of salvation, which is to know you, the only true God, and Jesus Christ whom you have sent. May those whom you have already visited with your grace, and enlightened by the knowledge of your Word, grow in all goodness, enriched by your spiritual blessing, so that together we may all worship you with heart and voice, giving honour and homage to Christ, our Master, King and Lawgiver.

Likewise, O God of all comfort, we commend to you all whom you visit and chastise with cross and tribulation, whether it be through poverty or prison, sickness or exile, or affliction of body or mind. May you make known to them your fatherly love, and assure them that their chastisement is for amendment of life. And may they with willing heart turn to you and, being converted, receive your comfort, being delivered from every distress.

Finally, O God and Father, grant also that we, who are gathered here in Jesus' name to hear his Word, may, without dissembling or hypocrisy, acknowledge that by nature we are lost, that we deserve your punishment, and daily heap up condemnation to ourselves by our wretched and unruly lives. Help us to see that in us there is nothing good, and that flesh and blood can never inherit your kingdom. May we gladly and with steadfast trust submit to our Lord Jesus Christ, our only Saviour and Redeemer. And may he so live in us that, our old Adam being put to death, we may rise to a new and better life, to the praise and glory of your name.

ABBREVIATIONS USED IN ENDNOTES

Ann.:   Erasmus, *Annotations on the New Testament: the Gospels* (ed. Anne Reeve), London: Duckworth, 1986.

Badius: Calvin, S*oixante cinq sermons sur l'Harmonie ou Concordance des trois Evangelistes*, Geneva: Conrad Badius, 1562.

CO: *J. Calvini opera quae supersunt omnia*, 59 vol. (ed. W. Baum, E. Cunitz and E. Reuss), Berlin & Brunswick: C. A. Schwetschke & Son, 1863–1900.

Harm.   *A Harmony of the Gospels: Calvin's New Testament Commentaries*, 3 vol. (ed. D. W. Torrance and T. F. Torrance, tr. A. W. Morrison and T. H. L. Parker), Edinburgh: St. Andrew Press, 1972.

Epistres: Lefèvre d'Etaples et ses disciples, *Epistres et Evangiles pour les cinquante et deux dimanches de l'an* (ed. G. Bedouelle and F. Giacone), Leiden: E. J. Brill, 1976.

Inst.   Calvin, *Institutes of the Christian Religion*, 2 vol. (ed. J. T. McNeill, tr. F. L. Battles), Philadelphia: Westminster Press, 1960.

LW   *Luther's Works*, 55 vol. (ed. J. Pelikan and H. T. Lehmann), St Louis: Concordia Publishing House and Philadelphia: Fortress Press, 1955–86.

NPNF   *A Select Library of the Nicene and Post-Nicene Fathers*, First series, 14 vol. (ed. Philip Schaff), New York: Scribner, 1886–89, repr. Peabody, Mass.: Hendrickson, 1995.

OS   *J. Calvini opera selecta*, 5 vol. (ed. P. Barth and W. Niesel), Munich: Kaiser, 1926–52.

| SC | *Supplementa calviniana: Sermons inédits de Jean Calvin,* 8 vol. to date, Neukirchen-Vluyn: Neukirchener Verlag, 1936/1961 –. |
| S. Chr. | *Sources chrétiennes* (ed. H. de Lubac, J. Daniélou et al.), 259 vol. to date, Paris: Editions du Cerf, 1942 –. |

ENDNOTES

SERMON 1

The Sixty-first Sermon of the Gospel Harmony.
Badius, pp. 1096–1113; *CO* 46.761–72.

For Calvin the Beatitudes begin, not with the first *makarioi* of *Matt.* 5:3, but with the calling of the earliest disciples. Grace is written into the Gospel narratives before ever Jesus begins to teach. The preacher is not so much concerned to depict the background against which the Beatitudes were spoken as the core audience to which they were addressed. There is a short linguistic gloss on the Aramaic expression 'sons of thunder' and on the name Peter/Cephas.

Calvin's overriding interest, however, is in the twin questions, 'What qualities did those who were called possess?' and 'Why were these men preferred above all others?' His answers are characteristically firm, and developed at some length. Christ's will alone accounts for his choice of the Twelve, a fact which makes any calculation of relative merit profitless. The disciples are presented as 'rough men', poorly educated, unlikely candidates for ultimate apostleship. But then, declares Calvin, not even the most gifted of men can satisfy God's standard of acceptability. We are all beggars, all equally dependent on God's indiscriminate kindness.

A brief consideration of Jesus at prayer is followed by a third and more troubling question, 'Why Judas Iscariot?' The answer is somewhat indirect, in that Calvin looks at the lessons to be learned from Judas' story. The figure of the betrayer illustrates the mixed nature of the church on earth. He stands as a warning to those who naively expect perfection in the church visible, as a spur to those who are easily discouraged by trouble and defections, and as a summons to the proud to take care lest they fall. Such an answer does not solve the moral problem of Judas' perdition: by implication, the solution lies beyond man's knowledge. Instead, the preacher hurries on to his closing theme – God's overriding prerogative. Whatever institutions God has established for the ordering of human affairs cannot fail, however much we may deride or pervert them. Human sin does not taint God nor frustrate his purposes. Sin in the church is assuredly deplorable; it does not, however, invalidate the gospel, nor does it make the preaching office superfluous. It is only by the Word made audible that the work of grace is carried forward.

[1] *the fifteenth chapter of St John. John* 15:16.

[2] *further than we should into his counsels.* In Calvin's view, God's self-disclosure in creation and in Scripture is sufficient to lead men to repentance and faith, and to make unbelief inexcusable. Neither general nor special revelation, however, exhausts the mystery of God's person and his hidden designs. Speculation is strongly discouraged: it is an unprofitable exercise, a fertile source of error, and a symptom of man's besetting sin – his intellectual pride. Cf. *Inst.* 3.23.8 (p. 957): 'Let us not be ashamed to submit our understanding to God's boundless wisdom so far as to yield before its many secrets. For, of those things which it is neither given nor lawful to know, ignorance is knowledge, and the craving to know is a kind of madness.' On inscrutability as a fundamental attribute of God, see Richard Stauffer, *Dieu, la création et la providence dans la prédication de Calvin* (Berne: Peter Lang, 1978), pp. 19-23; 109-10.

[3] *should return the favour. Job* 41:11. Cf. *Job* 35:7, quoted by Paul in *Rom.* 11:35.

[4] *as Psalm 16 says. Psa.* 16:2. The Hebrew is difficult, and has been rendered in a number of ways. Vulgate: 'May my judgment

come forth from before your face.' Lefèvre d'Etaples (*Quincuplex psalterium*, 1513) paraphrases: 'May just sentence come forth from the serenity of your countenance.' In his Commentary on *Psa.* 16:2, Calvin understands the verse to mean, 'The good I do does not extend to you' (*CO* 31. 149).

[5] *as I was saying this morning.* The sermon is thus an afternoon sermon. In the morning Calvin had preached on the miracles of healing recorded in *Matt.* 8:14–18, *Mark* 1:29–39 and *Luke* 4:38–43.

[6] *a more appropriate time.* A reference to *Matt.* 6:5–15 and parallels, which Calvin would probably have reached by the beginning of 1561. The passage is treated at some length in *Harm.* I, pp. 202–14.

[7] *back to life. John* 11:35.

[8] *St Paul uses to describe him.* Phil. 2:7. Cf. Commentary on *Phil.* 2:7, where Calvin renders the verse: 'He emptied himself' (*CO* 52. 26).

[9] *upon his knees before God.* In the case of David, Calvin may have had a verse such as *Psa.* 55:17 in mind. The reference to Paul is clearer, *Eph.* 3:14-15 (freely paraphrased).

[10] *as he would have been called.* An unusual linguistic note, intended perhaps to defend Scripture against the charge of textual inconsistency. The same point about the nickname, 'sons of thunder', is made in *Harm.* I, p. 167.

[11] *the whole world trembles. Hag.* 2:6–7, where not the gospel, but the restoration of the temple is in view.

[12] *the mountains to shake. Psa.* 29:3-9. It is clear from Calvin's remarks that the Psalm had been sung in the course of the service. By 1560, metrical versions of 83 Psalms were in use in Geneva's churches, with texts composed by Clément Marot and Théodore de Bèze (Beza). The Psalms were appointed to be sung in a prescribed order over a 28-week cycle, Psalm 29 being reserved for the second Sunday service in Week 6. See Pierre Pidoux, *Le Psautier huguenot* (Basel: Baerenreiter, 1962) II, pp. 61–62.

[13] *mixed with good grain. Matt.* 13:24–30 (threshing-floor), *Matt.* 13:47–48 (net of fishes). In context, both images illustrate, not the mixed nature of the church, but the eschatological themes of separation and judgment. On the visible church as a mixed fellowship of true and false believers, see *Inst.* 4.1.13–16 (pp. 1026–31), where Calvin's argument is directed in part against the Anabaptists' insistence on a strictly disciplined, separated and holy church.

[14] *be plainly revealed. 1 Cor.* 11:19.

[15] *to create the utmost mischief.* Calvin sometimes conflates biblical texts which are thematically related. Here, his reference to impostors appears to echo Jesus' strictures against the hypocrites in *Matt.* 6:2, 5, 16; on the other hand, the 'root of faith' which fails in time of trouble recalls the parable of the Sower (*Matt.* 13:21 and parallels).

[16] *he will sit in God's sanctuary. 2 Thess.* 2:4.

[17] *such men will come. Acts* 20:29–30.

[18] *second chapter of 2 Timothy is true. 2 Tim.* 2:19.

[19] *until the last day. John* 10:28, with perhaps a reminiscence of *John* 6:39.

[20] *should beware lest they fall. 1 Cor.* 10:12.

[21] *he is past all help.* In Calvin's hands, the popular proverb serves both to give colour to his style and to illustrate in a pithy and direct way a variety of moral dilemmas. Not all proverbs, however, meet, as this one does, with the preacher's approval. Others articulate a point of view diametrically opposed to his own, and are invoked only to be refuted. Cf. my article, '*Comme on dit*: the Proverb in Calvin's Sermons', *Journal of the Australasian Universities Language and Literature Association*, 88 (1997), pp. 71–82.

[22] *he was called a devil. John* 6:70.

[23] *propensity for evil.* As has often been remarked, Calvin has a high view of the ministry of Word and sacrament. The dignity,

however, which attaches to the office of minister or teaching elder is unconditional only in the sense that the Word proclaimed is God's, not man's, and that God, its author, chooses to use the most imperfect of human instruments to effect the work of grace. Such is Calvin's meaning when he speaks of the preacher as God's 'angel' or 'mouthpiece' (Sermon on *Deut.* 1:22-28; *CO* 25. 667), and of preaching as 'the place where Jesus Christ resides and has his royal seat' (Sermon on *1 Cor.* 11:4-10; *CO* 49. 734-5). It is not a dignity inherent in the holders of the office who, as Calvin recognizes, may by their doctrine, motive or manner of life forfeit any claim to be pastors of God's flock. See further, on the importance and dignity of the pastorate, *Inst.* 4.1.5-6 (pp. 1016-21); 4.3.1-3 (pp. 1053-6); and Alexandre Ganoczy, *Calvin, théologien de l'Eglise et du ministère* (Paris: Ed. du Cerf, 1964), pp. 333-7; 344-53.

SERMON 2

The Sixty-second Sermon of the Gospel Harmony.
Badius, pp. 1113-29; *CO* 46.771-84.

The first two Beatitudes anticipate Jesus' teaching, in *Matt.* 16:24 and parallels, on the cost of discipleship. The imagery employed is, for Calvin, as explicit and unambiguous as any discourse on sacrifice and suffering could be. It is, however, with the notion of blessedness that he begins. Among the various definitions offered by philosophers, none is found to be satisfactory, since none is able to reconcile the pursuit of happiness with that most fundamental of human experiences, affliction. Affliction is what Christ first promises his disciples, together with a blessedness beyond human comprehension. Those who in the first two Beatitudes are afflicted are the poor, the poor 'in spirit' and the grieving. Unlike other commentators, Calvin does not spend time distinguishing one term from another: all, in his view, represent the idea of suffering, deserved or undeserved, and all designate the brokenness which comes, not from superior spiritual aspiration, but from the experience of pain, disgrace, calamity. To be poor, to grieve, to be hungry, is not to long for a righteousness which we do not have, but, more simply, to cry to God for help and deliverance when every human prop – companionship, esteem, health, and material comfort – has disappeared. The preacher is not naive enough to believe that affliction is always salutary: it can harden the sufferer, just as wealth can harden the rich. Nor does he recommend that the Christian seek out affliction as a way of life: that is the way of the masochist, or of the ascetic who endeavours to purge his own sin.

But affliction can assuredly be a gift, one which works better results than prosperity, its opposite. It teaches a strict but vital lesson: the necessity for a hope which looks beyond this passing world to a salvation reserved for us in heaven. 'It is enough that God loves us', says the preacher. 'By faith we lay hold of that love when we leave this world.' The promises, then, of a kingdom, of consolation, of satisfaction, are for those who, in violation of the instinct for self-reliance, reach out in their distress to God. God the unmovable is moved by our tears.

There is pathos here, but no sentimentality. Victory comes only after defeat, in the midst of defeat, victory won through the sufferings of the Son of man. In bringing his sermon to an end, Calvin is at pains to stress that most singular and – for people in every age – most uncomfortable of truths: the way of blessedness is the way of the Cross.

[1] *to acquire superior learning.* Calvin's comment on the redundant expression, 'opening his mouth, he taught', is not unlike his comment in the preceding sermon on 'sons of thunder'. In this case a note on language serves to demonstrate the authenticity of the

Gospel record. Cf. Augustine, *Our Lord's Sermon on the Mount* (*NPNF* 6, p. 4): 'He is said to have opened his own mouth, whereas under the old law he was accustomed to open the mouths of the prophets.'

[2] *we attain supreme happiness.* As a humanist, Calvin was thoroughly conversant with classical definitions of the happy life. Among the Roman writers, Cicero and Seneca would have provided a ready source of reference. In general, the opinions which the Reformer canvasses reflect the varying emphases of the Epicureans (pursuit of pleasure, avoidance of pain) and of the Stoics (cultivation of virtue, both individual and civic). The idea that 'we should behave properly', and that 'virtue is nurtured by contentment', echoes Aristotle (*Nicomachean Ethics*, I.vii.9-viii.14), who taught that the key to correct behaviour lay in the application of moral knowledge to concrete situations. For Aristotle the good life consisted not so much in virtue as in its active exercise, which for those who practised it was invariably a source of pleasure. The notion of correct behaviour cannot, however, be confined to one school of thought. It might well include Cicero's ideal of 'decorum', of honourable conduct appropriate to the context (*De officiis*, I.xxvii.93-5; cf. *De finibus*, V.ix.24-6).

[3] *the school of our Lord Jesus Christ.* Over thirty years earlier, Lefèvre and his collaborators had described the general thrust of the Beatitudes in similar terms (*Epistres* 66B, p. 373): 'If ever folly existed in the eyes of men, it is in this Gospel passage. How could the world comprehend that poverty can be wealth or death, life? That war can be peace and sadness, joy? . . . As St Paul testifies, this world has nothing in common with Christ. Whenever did the world's sages and philosophers conceive of such happiness as divine wisdom reveals to us here? . . . The teaching of this text belongs only to Christians, in whose heart Jesus Christ, his cross, his truth and Word are truly planted.'

[4] *fit the context.* Calvin takes issue here with a long exegetical tradition which equates 'poverty in spirit' with self-abasement or self-denial. For Jerome, the poor in spirit are those who, led by the Spirit, have voluntarily made themselves humble (Commentary on *Matt.* 5:3; *S.Chr.* 242, pp. 104–5). Chrysostom defines them as 'the contrite . . . the awestruck who tremble at God's commands' (*Homily XV on St Matthew*, *NPNF* 10, p. 92). Erasmus agrees, and cites Augustine to the same effect (*Ann.*, p. 25). Luther sets the spiritually poor over against the 'rich bellies' who trust in temporal goods; for him, the poor are those who behave as those who have nothing; they are ready at any time to give up everything for God's sake (*Sermon on the Mount*, *LW* 21, pp. 13–15).

Calvin does not deny the importance of inner disposition, but sees it as the consequence of various trials which destroy all pride and throw us back upon God. He views the poor in spirit, not as those who are humble in themselves, but as those who have been humbled by events.

[5] *passage to which we will later come.* A variety of passages suggest themselves, chief among them the narrative of Jesus and the rich young ruler (*Matt.* 19:16–22 and parallels), and the parable of the Pharisee and the publican (*Luke* 18:9–14).

[6] *the lowly and the once despised. Luke* 1:52. The Reformer had expounded this verse in the eleventh and twelfth sermons of the *Gospel Harmony.*

[7] *no more than a penny.* The reference is to the use of chips or counters for tallying points gained or money won in games of chance. The fact that gambling was banned in Geneva gives the analogy added irony. The related image of the tennis ball hit back and forth across the *jeu de paume* is often used by Calvin to parody the belief that providence is capricious or erratic. Cf. Sermons on *Job* 5:11–15; 12:17–25 (*CO* 33. 246, 594); Sermons on *Jer.* 18:1–10 (*SC* 6, pp. 141, 145); Sermon on *1 Cor.* 10:7 (*CO* 49. 617).

[8] *something we can see. Rom.* 5:3 (paraphrased), with *Rom.* 8:24.

[9] *difficult to digest.* On the metaphor of food chewed prior to digestion, see Sermon on *Psa.* 119 (*CO* 32. 483) and Sermon on *Job* 8:7–13 (*CO* 33. 387). Cf. Sermon on *Eph.* 6:19–24: 'Although we have the Word preached to us and chewed over, so to speak, for us simply to swallow, we nevertheless remain senseless like blocks of wood, until God enlightens us by his Holy Spirit' (*CO* 51. 856–7). On this and other aspects of the divine pedagogy, see Ford Lewis Battles, 'God was Accommodating Himself to Human Capacity', *Interpretation* 31 (1977), pp. 19–38.

[10] *so to speak, dead men.* Again, the Reformer departs from the reading preferred by the Fathers, who generally assume that mourning for sins is what is meant. Thus Hilary of Poitiers: 'It is not because we mourn the loss of loved ones, insults, or wrongs, it is because we mourn our former sins and keenly feel the enormity of our crimes, that consolation is carefully laid up for us in heaven' (*On Matthew* 4.4, *S. Chr.* 254, pp. 124–5). Augustine is something of an exception: 'Mourning is sorrow arising from the loss of things held dear; but those who are converted to God lose those things which in this world they were accustomed to embrace as dear . . . Until the love of eternal things is born in them, they are wounded by some measure of grief.' (*Our Lord's Sermon on the Mount, NPNF* 6, p. 22).

[11] *evil-doers are oppressing us.* Calvin does not favour the view that the suffering which Christians experience is necessarily a proof of their merit ('virtue'), or the result of external oppression. Personal frailty, imprudence, recklessness, and self-will all contribute to the sum of individual misery. What the Reformer consistently teaches is that suffering is the means whereby God tempers and trains Christian character, making it more like Christ's, and weaning those who are his from love of this world. 'Believers, . . . warned by proofs of their infirmities, advance toward

humility and so, sloughing off perverse confidence in the flesh, betake themselves to God's grace' (*Inst.* 3.8.2, p. 703).

[12] *my tears in a bottle. Psa.* 56:8. In his earlier commentary on the verse (*CO* 31. 550), Calvin had preferred the imperative: 'Put my tears . . .'

SERMON 3

The Sixty-third Sermon of the Gospel Harmony.
Badius, pp. 1130–49; *CO* 46.783–98.

In no sermon is the contrast more sharply drawn between theory and practice, between claim and performance. Nor does any sermon express a Christian social ethic more all-embracing than this. Calvin laments the loss of mutual respect and solidarity which should prevail among all who bear God's image. We are ruled by anarchic self-love, however much we might vaunt the ideals of tolerance and philanthropy. A fallen world has therefore little use for meekness and mercy. Experience and common sense alike suggest that victory goes to the ruthless and the ambitious – an illusory victory, the preacher assures his hearers, which will sooner or later turn to ashes.

Not utopianism, but God's quality of justice, explains the Reformer's belief that retribution will overtake the oppressor. In the meantime, however, there are the oppressed, those who suffer for – the qualification is important – righteousness' sake. Unlike his exposition of the first two Beatitudes, where the emphasis was on the fruit of tribulation – brokenness – Calvin focuses here on suffering as a wrong visited upon those who are in the right, on affliction undeserved, on distress which falls upon the innocent. The innocent are the meek who do not retaliate when unfairly attacked, who endure the world's malice, not because they see no evil but because patience is the pattern they have learned from Christ – Christ who is a Shepherd not of wolves but of sheep. The innocent are also the hungry and thirsty who have suffered loss in the defence of a just and worthy cause. They *may* hunger and thirst for righteousness, but that is not how Calvin reads the text. Hunger and thirst are the penalty they pay for their failure to turn a blind eye to injustice in all its forms. By their suffering they demonstrate that there exists a standard of equity by which all men are, even now, being judged. The innocent are, finally, the merciful, who by their compassion challenge the cold emotion we call charity and the economic exploitation which passes for good business. To be merciful is to practise a costly altruism which springs from the heart. Altruism may also represent wasted effort, as the preacher candidly admits, since gratitude is a commodity in short supply. Believers are nevertheless not discouraged.

Necessity compels them: by virtue of a common creation they are bound up with their fellows in the same bundle; and by virtue of an uncommon redemption they have received mercy which is freely offered to all. The summons to be merciful is thus doubly rooted in theology – triply, if we hearken to Calvin's conclusion, which moves from creation to redemption and from redemption to final judgment. If the meek, the hungry, the thirsty, and the merciful are blessed, it is because judgment with mercy will be given to those who, debtors to mercy, have lived by Christ's rule of love, and await its consummation in heaven.

[1] *someone else's dinner.* Two proverbs, each of which reflects a 'common-sense' point of view at variance with Christ's teaching. Both recur in much the same form in Commentary on *Matt.* 5:5 (p. 170). To 'run with the hare and hunt with the hounds' (French: 'to howl with the wolves') is an expression frequently found in Calvin when he wishes to warn against the perils of conformity. See, e.g.,

Commentary on *Gen.* 6:9 (*CO* 23. 120); and Sermons on *Jer.* 17:11–14 *(SC* 6, p. 114); *Mic.* 7:4-7 (*SC* 5, p. 220); *Gal.* 6:2–5 (*CO* 51. 75); *1 Tim.* 6:13–16 (*CO* 53. 616).

[2] *as the prophet himself declares. Isa.* 57:20.

[3] *what could I do? Deut.* 28:65–67 (paraphrased).

[4] *as Psalm 37 says. Psa.* 37:9–11.

[5] *overcome evil with good.* The quotation is from Paul, *Rom.* 12:21. Calvin may be thinking of Jesus' teaching elsewhere in the Sermon on the Mount, *Matt.* 5:38–48.

[6] *revived and restored.* A reference perhaps to passages such as *Rom.* 8:21–23 and *1 Pet.* 1:5. Calvin is reluctant to interpret the promise of 'earth' in too literal or immediate a sense. Cf. Luther, for whom the promise may be realized here and now, in the enjoyment of land, home, family, and possessions (*Sermon on the Mount, LW* 21, p. 22). Chrysostom speaks of both a present ('sensible') and future ('spiritual') realization (*Homily XV on St Matthew, NPNF* 10, pp. 93–4). For Lefèvre and his circle, the promise is wholly future: 'the holy city on high, paradise' (*Epistres* 66B, p. 374).

[7] *meaning can be derived.* Calvin is perhaps thinking of Augustine's gloss: 'He calls them lovers of a true and indestructible good' (*Our Lord's Sermon on the Mount, NPNF* 6, p. 23). Jerome interprets similarly: 'It is not enough for us to desire righteousness, unless we hunger for it, a metaphor which teaches us that we are never righteous enough but must always hunger for the works of righteousness' (Commentary on *Matt.* 5:6, *S. Chr.* 242, pp. 106–7). Cf. Hilary: 'The hunger of the saints for the teaching of God will be crowned with the gift of perfect satisfaction in heaven' (*On Matthew* 4:5, *S. Chr.* 254, pp. 124–5).

[8] *they will be filled.* Two themes are intertwined here: the Christian's motive for well-doing, and the rights of the persecuted believer. In the first place, the preacher affirms that Christians do not refrain from harming others in order to win approval or to gain

some moral or material advantage for themselves. Their conduct is not calculated to deceive; they do not employ underhand or illicit means to get their way. They seek to do good because God himself is good.

In the second place, the duty to do good does not require believers to surrender their right to equitable treatment and to freedom from oppression. If they are innocent, their innocence deserves to be recognized and protected. Unmerited persecution may – indeed, will – be the Christian's lot. However it is never, in Calvin's eyes, something to be silently accepted. It remains an anomaly, a scandal to be deplored, condemned, and, if possible, corrected.

[9] *as St Paul exhorts us to do. Rom.* 12:15.

[10] *chapter 2 of his Epistle.* The reference is to the problem of faith without works, *James* 2:14-17.

[11] *the burden of humanity.* Calvin consistently represents God as supremely generous to a fallen world. God's pity is such that, through the operation of common or general grace, wickedness is restrained, and human beings enabled to exercise among themselves a degree of benevolence, civic responsibility, and even virtue, belied by their status as unregenerate sinners. Cf. *Inst.* 2.2.17 (pp. 276-7) and 2.3.3 (pp. 292-3).

[12] *the measure we have given. Matt.* 7:2. Cf. *Harm. Matt.* 7:1 (pp. 225-6): 'Whoever judges by the law and Word of God, and directs his judgment by the rule of charity, always begins his censure with himself, and this preserves in judgment a proper limit and order . . . A penalty is pronounced upon those rigid critics who are so busy in shaking out others' sins: they will be treated with no more humanity by others, but will feel the same severity against themselves as they exercised upon others.'

[13] *judged without mercy. James.* 2:13.

[14] *chapter 18 of St John's Gospel.* A lapse of memory, or transcription error? *John* 1:18 is meant.

[15] *precious things they possessed. Exod.* 12:36.

[16] *Christ's precious blood.* In his sermons, Calvin sometimes adopts, as here, the naive observer's point of view. Geneva being an avowedly Christian society, its members might, broadly speaking, be regarded as brethren, with an equal claim to God's work of grace in Christ. Displays of animosity effectively denied the faith which all professed to hold. A similar situation is envisaged in Sermon 4 (see footnote 7).

[17] *those who are sinners like you.* The reference appears to be an amalgam of several Pauline passages: *2 Cor.* 2:7–8; *Gal.* 6:1; *1 Tim.* 5:20–21.

[18] *between now and Sunday.* Ministerial movements in Geneva and its dependent territories were proposed by the Company of Pastors and submitted to the Small Council (essentially, the city government) for approval. The 1541 Ecclesiastical Ordinances provided for congregational consent when ministers were to be inducted into a new charge, but the system had fallen into abeyance until revived by resolution of the Council of Two Hundred in Feb. 1560 (*OS* II, pp. 330–1; *CO* 10.17–18, 94). Hence the Reformer's reference to the 'rights' of all church members. The minister, whose arrival is announced here, was Pierre d'Airebaudouze, *sieur* of Anduse, son of a noble family from the Languedoc region of France. Pastor since 1555 of the outlying parish of Jussy, his removal to Geneva had been proposed by Calvin on 14 Oct. 1560; by 11 Nov. he had taken up residence in the city (*CO* 21. 736, 738). See further Robert M. Kingdon and Jean-François Bergier (eds.), *Registres de la Compagnie des pasteurs de Genève au temps de Calvin* (Geneva: Droz, 1962–4) II, pp. 64, 93–4, and the entry in E. and E. Haag, *La France protestante*, 2nd ed. (Paris: Sandoz & Fischbacher, 1877–8) I, pp. 19–20.

SERMON 4

The Sixty-fourth Sermon of the Gospel Harmony.
Badius, pp. 1150–67; *CO* 46.797–810.

[Calvin here expounds *Matt.* 5:8–10, to the virtual exclusion of *Luke* 6:22–23. He deals with the latter text in the following sermon.]

To be pure in heart is not to be sinless or to have reached perfection; it is to be transparently honest in all one says and does. It is, to use Calvin's metaphor, to follow the straight rather than the sinuous line, to renounce deceit and the manipulative tricks by which people seek their best advantage. The pure in heart do not 'see' what is good for them; they are blind to all that would hide God's face from them. An ironic counterpoint is thus set up between the vision of the pure in heart and that of the worldly-minded, an irony directed not only against the clever and unscrupulous but against the insatiably curious who would know more of God's secrets than is lawful for them.

It is, however, the next Beatitude, concerning peace and peace-making, which particularly interests the preacher. A useful distinction is made between peaceableness of disposition and peaceableness of action, and leads to a sustained plea for the believer to abstain from injuring others – a quality also of the meek and merciful, since nothing in the Beatitudes is quite water-tight – and, more positively, to extinguish the flames of hatred once they are lit. Only so can we show ourselves to be children of the heavenly Father, who is the author of peace. Nevertheless, Calvin is not an apologist for indiscriminate peace, for that would be to place the aggressor and the victim, the bad and the good, on an equal footing. A permanent truce is not an option where there are wrongs to be righted. To insist on just outcomes is, however, to accept the necessity of combat and the certainty of persecution. For when battle is joined with the wrongdoer much suffering ensues for God's people, and never more so than when the battle is for God's truth and Christ's gospel, for the recognition, that is, that God's will should govern the life of society and that Christ's atonement alone can renew it.

The Christian thus suffers twice over: as a human being, caught up in his own and others' quarrels, and as a believer, harried by the devil and by those who do his work. But suffering is not a badge which all can wear: only those who suffer 'for righteousness' sake' are promised blessing. Through many tribulations, not all of them of our own making, we enter the kingdom of heaven. We enter, of course, not as the deserving, but because grace has preceded us.

In concluding his sermon, Calvin reminds his hearers that God sought us betimes, while we were still estranged from him, and gave us a Saviour when we looked for none. Jesus Christ is the great Peace-maker. His act of reconciliation makes it possible for us to be reconciled with one another. The price of peace is a price worth paying, for it is a price already paid.

[1] *profit from someone else's loss.* While some of Calvin's strictures resemble those he makes elsewhere against the 'spiritual' Libertines who lead believers astray by clever argument and by the appearance of piety, the picture he paints here is of human deviousness in all its forms. Sharp business practices as well as private and public deceits are included in his condemnation. Cf. Luther, who considers the pure in heart to be the converted, those who have the Word of God and faith, and who love all that God commands. Much of Luther's comment on this verse is directed against monasticism and its horror of contamination by the world (*Sermon on the Mount, LW* 21, pp. 32–9).

² *the Father in heaven. Matt.* 18:10. On Calvin's doctrine of the angels and their function, see his long discussion in *Inst.* 1.14.4–12 (pp. 163–72).

³ *as St John says in his first Epistle. 1 John* 3:2.

⁴ *what God has prepared for us. 1 Cor.* 2:9, echoing *Isa.* 64:4.

⁵ *a composite one: 'peace' and 'make'.* Greek ειρενοποιοι; cf. Latin *pacifici.*

⁶ *unless we lead by example.* The notion that peace must begin with the peace-maker is found in earlier commentators. It is particularly prominent in Jerome: 'Blessed are the peace-makers, who cause peace to reign first in their hearts, then among the separated brethren. What is the point of promoting peace among others if the various vices are at war in the heart?' (Commentary on *Matt.* 5:9, *S. Chr.* 242, pp. 106–9). Cf. Erasmus' ironic lament: 'Such sentiments, given the way most men behave, are like songs sung to the deaf' (*Ann.*, p. 26). Lefèvre interprets the command to make peace as a pressing call to conversion through the preaching of the gospel: 'We must above all attain peace with God, which is effected when we proclaim his holy Word' (*Epistres* 66 B, p. 376).

⁷ *Two people at odds.* See Sermon 3, note 16.

⁸ *rightly called the God of peace. Rom.* 15:33; 16:20; *Phil.* 4:9; *Heb.* 13:20.

⁹ *as St Paul urges us. Rom.* 12:18; 14:9; *1 Thess.* 5:13.

¹⁰ *suffer . . . for the gospel's sake.* The Reformers and their supporters were frequently accused of creating civil disturbance and fomenting insurrection against lawful authority. Calvin's letter of 1535 to Francis I, which prefaces every edition of the *Institutes*, directly addresses the issue. In it he defends the peaceful intentions of all true believers, and argues that discord is the work of Satan, aided and abetted by the enemies of the gospel who, as in the time of the prophets and apostles, 'contend against God's power' (*Inst.*, pp. 27–30). In his exposition of *Matt.* 5:12, Luther makes the same

point: 'How could things run smoothly when the devil is in charge
and is a mortal enemy of the gospel? ... If he is to resist and hinder
it, he must rally all his art and power and arouse everything in his
might against it' (*Sermon on the Mount*, *LW* 21, p. 52).

[11] *who are powerful among men.* If, for the Reformer, poverty
confers no automatic moral advantage on the poor, wealth brings
with it a terrible potential for abuse, especially when allied with
political power. Calvin's general teaching on poverty and wealth is
outlined by Ronald S. Wallace, *Calvin's Doctrine of the Christian
Life* (London & Edinburgh: Oliver & Boyd, 1959), pp. 126–8, 152–
4, 176–7, 185–6. On the injustices inherent in a society where wealth
and power are in the hands of one or only a few, see Harro Höpfl,
The Christian Polity of John Calvin (Cambridge: The University
Press, 1982), pp. 160–71.

[12] *who can be your enemy? 1 Pet.* 3:13.

[13] *must expect persecution. 2 Tim.* 3:12.

[14] *the devil's children, as they are.* The demonizing of opponents,
a procedure not unknown in our own day, was common currency
in sixteenth-century debate. By 1560 Calvin could look back over
a long series of attempts to engineer a doctrinal accord between
Roman Catholics and Protestants. All had proved abortive,
although there remained in evangelical circles those – often styled
by Calvin as *moyenneurs* or 'mediators' – who continued to believe
that the break was not irreparable. The Reformer had no such
hopes. See on this question, Richard Stauffer, 'Calvin et le *De offi-
cio pii ac publicae tranquillitatis vere amantis viri*', *Interprètes de la
Bible* (Paris: Beauchesne, 1980), pp. 249–67.

[15] *who suffer persecution.* The term 'Anabaptist' denotes a range of
dissenting movements on the margins of mainstream Protestantism, from the militant Münsterites to the pacifist Swiss and South
German Brethren. It was the latter with whom Calvin had most to
do. Their belief (already noted) in a separated church of saints,

their refusal to bear arms, swear oaths or occupy public office, their rejection of infant baptism and their strict enforcement of the ban (excommunication), made them a target for persecution in both Catholic and Protestant lands. The Sermon on the Mount exercised a strong influence on the Anabaptist view of the holy life, as Luther notes in the preface to his exposition (*LW* 21, p. 5). Luther, like Calvin, regarded the Anabaptist insistence on perfection as both unbalanced and schismatic. See further Willem Balke, *Calvin and the Anabaptist Radicals*, trans. William Heynen (Grand Rapids: Eerdmans, 1981).

[16] *their iniquities, not for themselves. Psa.* 139:21–22. In his earlier commentary on the Psalms, Calvin had taken care to draw the same distinction between hatred of sin and love of the sinner (*CO* 32.385–6). *Psa.* 139 itself makes no such distinction.

[17] *maintaining brotherhood among us. 1 Cor.* 3:3; *Eph.* 2:14–16; *Titus* 3:9.

[18] *no one upholds truth. Isa.* 59:4, with *Isa.* 59:14.

SERMON 5

The Sixty-fifth and last recorded sermon of the Gospel Harmony.
Badius, pp. 1168–89; *CO* 46.809–26.

The last sermon on the Beatitudes is a summation of all that Calvin has said before on the subject of undeserved suffering. Here, suffering is set in the context of persecution. To be committed to God's truth is to invite persecution, especially when truth is at odds with cherished church tradition and entrenched authority. If one excepts the preacher's protest against Rome's capricious use of excommunication, there are no topical allusions, no list of Protestant martyrs who, braving the world, the flesh and the devil, were faithful unto death. The prophets and apostles are held up as sufficient models for imitation. It is striking to see how often Calvin represents persecution in the form, not of physical distress – exile, beatings, imprisonment – but of verbal abuse, ill-report, and vilification. Striking, too, is the response he recommends to his hearers: unhurried perseverance in the path appointed by the Father. Persecuted believers do not run toward the kingdom; they walk, if need be they limp and shuffle, each step supported and directed by the Spirit, the Comforter.

Jesus' promise of reward to the persecuted gives rise to a lively discussion of works and grace, grace and merit. Although he does not explicitly cite Augustine, the preacher's argument is cast in the Augustinian mould: good works are 'ours' only in so far as they are given to us; only those who forsake their own merits can live the life pleasing to God and receive the blessings which Christ has obtained.

The woes, which in Luke are pronounced upon the rich, pose the timely question of the proper use of this world's goods. All good things, says Calvin, are gifts from God and are meant to lead us in gratitude to the Giver. But to accept the Giver is to accept all his gifts without exception, including the severe gift (for such it is) of affliction. By a roundabout route the Reformer thus returns to what throughout this series has been his grand theme: only through patience and tribulation can we reach the promised glory. The sermon concludes appropriately on a note of caution. To be well spoken of is of dubious benefit. Flattery is the way the world rewards its own: adulation traps the unwary and corrupts both ministers and laity. The preacher sees his warning as one which is profitable to all Christian people. Only by seeking Christ's commendation can the church, and the believers who are its living members, defend the integrity of the gospel message, enjoy its benefits, and confidently proclaim it to a needy world.

[1] *as our Lord himself says. John.* 3:20.

[2] *shame and dishonour among men.* The idea that death was preferable to public shame or disgrace was a commonplace among the classical poets and philosophers. A good name was the only lasting memorial a person might leave to posterity. So Aeschylus: 'If someone should suffer misfortune, let it be misfortune without dishonour, for that alone counts as gain among the dead' (*Seven against Thebes*, II.683–4).

Chrysostom develops the theme at some length in his *Homily XV on St Matthew*: 'Most assuredly, men's evil reports have a sharper bite than their deeds. For whereas, in our dangers, there are many things that lighten the toil, such as to be cheered by all, to have many applaud . . . and proclaim our praise, here, in our reproach, even this consolation is destroyed' (*NPFN* 10, p. 96).

[3] *men will spit in our face.* A probable reference to *1 Cor.* 4:11–12.

[4] *a most pleasing sacrifice. John* 16:2.

[5] *the eighth chapter of Isaiah. Isa.* 8:18.

[6] *in that kingdom, as in Judah.* Calvin holds that God's covenant with Israel was not abrogated by Israel's unfaithfulness, nor by the division of Solomon's kingdom into two and the installation of a rival cult in Bethel and Dan.

The idea of a believing remnant appears in both major and minor prophets, and is an important element in Calvin's covenant theology. It explains his belief in the preservation of Christ's church in the post-apostolic era, when ignorance, error, and apostasy threatened at times to extinguish God's truth.

The survival of the remnant (Latin: *residui* or *reliquiae*), the continuance of what Calvin sometimes calls the 'hidden seed' (Commentary on *Ezek.* 16:53; *CO* 40.387), is for him proof of God's vigilant care of the elect. The theme features prominently in his polemical exchanges with Roman Catholic opponents, who accused Protestantism of being a 'new' and therefore worthless religion. See Prefatory letter to Francis I, *Inst.* (pp. 14–16) and 3.21.7 (pp. 930–1).

[7] *odious and defiled.* Calvin's quarrel is not with the principle of excommunication (that is, exclusion from the fellowship of the Lord's Supper), whose pattern he finds in *Matt.* 18:15–17, but with the Church of Rome's practice. In the hands of the papal hierarchy, he declares, excommunication has become an instrument of arbitrary power, rather than a pastoral aid to correction and healing.

See the long discussion in *Inst.* 4.12.1–13, and my article, 'Oil and Vinegar: Calvin on Church Discipline', *Scottish Journal of Theology* 38 (1985), pp. 25–40.

[8] *as Scripture says in another place. Psa.* 37:6.

[9] *anything that men could bring against him. Jer.* 20:11–12.

[10] *as we will later see. Matt.* 6:2. Cf. *Harm. Matt.* 6:2 (p. 201): 'Christ is right to say that they have their reward now, who make this kind of show, for they cannot have eyes for God, whose sight is so full of vanity.'

[11] *whose sight Jesus restored. John* 9:1–38.

[12] *as St Peter says. 1 Pet.* 3:16 (paraphrased).

[13] *not grow tired of doing good. Gal.* 6:9, repeated in *2 Thess.* 3:13.

[14] *every possible indignity.* The preacher no doubt has in mind such passages as *Jer.* 26:7–11; 37:11–15; 38:4–6.

[15] *found in St Peter. 2 Pet.* 2:1–2.

[16] *the Psalm we have sung.* The reference is to the metrical version of *Psa.* 73, which was appointed to be sung in Week 10 of the 28-week cycle: stanzas 1–9 (verses 1–18) in the Sunday morning service, and stanzas 10–14 (verses 19–28) in the afternoon (Pierre Pidoux, *Le Psautier huguenot, II*, p. 62). The existence of the 28-week Psalm cycle makes it possible to establish in broad terms the chronology of the sermon series. An interval of exactly four weeks separates Sermon 1 (Week 6 of the cycle) from Sermon 5 (Week 10).

[17] *those who have served him well.* That salvation and its subsequent fruits are God's free gift, to be received by faith, was the cornerstone of Reformation theology. Calvin contrasts gratuitous grace with the Roman Catholic doctrine of works added to grace. The Council of Trent, in its sixth session (Jan. 1547), held that the grace of justification may be increased through the observance of good works joined to faith, works being a duty commanded by God and not simply a sign of justification (Chs. 10 and 11). Eternal life was defined both as a gift offered through Jesus Christ and as a reward paid to meritorious works (Ch. 16). Canon 32 sums up the Church's teaching thus: 'If anyone says that the good works of the justified man are in such a manner the gifts of God that they are not also the good merits of the justified man himself, or that the justified man through the good works which are done by him through the grace of God and the merits of Jesus Christ . . . does not truly merit an increase of grace, eternal life, and the obtaining of eternal life itself, provided he has died in grace, and also an increase of glory, let him be anathema' (H. Denzinger, *Enchiridion symbolorum*, Barcinone: Herder, 1957, pp. 289–95, 299). Calvin rebuts these propositions in his *Acts of the Council of Trent with the Antidote* (*CO* 7.457–9; 471–3; 485–6).

[18] *walking in his fear.* The first reference is to *Gal.* 6:10, the second, probably, to *1 Pet.* 2:12 with *1 Pet.* 3:16.

[19] *the good things in this present life.* Calvin's classic statement on the subject is found in *Inst.* 3.10.1–6 (pp. 719–25).

[20] *should we not also receive the bad? Job.* 2:10.

[21] *should be as those who have not. 1 Cor.* 7:30 (paraphrased).

[22] *as we read in Psalm 16. Psa.* 16:11.

[23] *would have to renounce God. Gal.* 1:10.

[24] *who come in the name of the Lord. Psa.* 118:26.

INDEX OF SCRIPTURE REFERENCES